THE
WEIGHT
OF
LEADERSHIP

Praise for *The Weight of Leadership*

I have read and enjoyed Ed Khouri's books for years. God trained him to show you the way.

—**Dr. Robert R. Perkinson,**
Author, *Chemical Dependency Counseling*

Something was missing in everything I had heard and read about leadership and codependency until I heard Ed. Shed the weight you were not meant to carry. You must read and apply *The Weight of Leadership.*

—**Dr. E. James Wilder,**
Neurotheologian, Co-author, *The Life Model*

Living through a pandemic, if we're honest, we've all found ourselves under the exhaustive weight of leadership, struggling in co-dependent ways we didn't even realize. The Weight of Leadership is a jewel; it's a must-read for ministry leaders and workers. Wisdom and experience are evident on every page as you discover how to lead from a better place. Ed's thought-provoking, honest, insightful work gives hope to the weary and invites health to the leader.

—**Dr. Brad Hoffmann,**
Pastor, Cool Spring Baptist Church, Mechanicsville, VA
Co-author, *Preventing Ministry Failure*
Co-host, the REimagine Podcast

The book you hold in your hand is a must-read for any leader who wants to go the distance. Ed Khouri has done it again. Through a keen understanding of neuroscience and many years of hands-on experience and research in emotional health, Ed lays out for us leaders a better way - a way that operates from a place of grace, with healthy attachments to God and others, and out of the true self. Do yourself a favor before you hit burnout and blow up your marriage or other relationships around you, and allow yourself to dive deeply into the message of this book. Become a grace-based leader that finishes well.

—Cathy Little,
Co-Founder and Director, Face to Face Ministries
facetofaceministries.org

I wish Ed Khouri could have written this book in the 1990s. Maybe if Ed had come to me and said, "you have to read this and live this"? But then, probably not. My thirty-something self wouldn't have understood this book AT ALL.

I unwittingly followed a self-motivated leadership path, assuming it was my job to figure out how to lead and grow our church and avoid the shame of failure. I carried a weight that I was not meant to carry alone.

There was a better, more restful way, and *The Weight of Leadership* shows it. Chapter 8 alone is worth the price of the whole book. I love these gems:

- "…God says quieting and rest are the *first* place to go— this is where we were designed to live." I didn't know how to quiet myself for the eleven years I lead that church.

- "When enemies are approaching, it is natural to want to make plans. The pressure can be overwhelming." Yes, under that intense pressure, I only knew to work harder.
- "Remembering that more horsepower doesn't guarantee God's power." I had bought the lie of "if it is to be, it is up to me." I forgot my own theology and plunged into the never-ending cycle of ministry production.

What to do now? I can't turn back the clock, but I can enthusiastically endorse this book, especially for those beginning the leadership journey. May this book become required reading in colleges and seminaries worldwide.

—Ray Woolridge,
Brigadier General (Retired), US Army
executive director, Life Model Works

I wholeheartedly endorse *The Weight of Leadership* and recommend it as an invaluable resource for ministry leaders—especially young, gifted and godly pastors. Indeed, you saved the best for last as the last chapter "puts it all together."

—John Mark Lamb
Consultant, Cru City

THE
WEIGHT
OF
LEADERSHIP

HOW CODEPENDENCY AND
MISPLACED MERCY UNDERMINE
LIFE AND MINISTRY

ED KHOURI

Foreword by Mindy Caliguire

ILLUMIFY
MEDIA.COM

THE
WEIGHT
OF
LEADERSHIP

The views and opinions expressed in this book are those of the author and do not necessarily reflect the official policy or position of Illumify Media Global.

Published by
Illumify Media Global
www.IllumifyMedia.com
"Let's bring your book to life!"

Library of Congress Control Number: 2022906365

Paperback ISBN: 978-1-955043-70-0

Typeset by Art Innovations (http://artinnovations.in/)
Cover design by Debbie Lewis

Printed in the United States of America

Dedication

To the next generation of leaders—old hands and greenhorns—
who will love through their fears, suffer well in trials,
and lead us into an unknown, but grace-filled future.

Contents

Foreword

True leadership is not so easy to find. Yet, on some level, there is a leader within us all. Whether we lead a family, an organization, a small group, or a worship team, we carry influence into the people and world around us. We lead, whether we intend to lead or not…and inevitably, something in our experience has formed *how* we "show up" in our role. But what if that way we are leading is off? What if our style of relating to those we lead works against God's vision of who our team and we become? What if the weight we carry is crushing our very souls or the souls of those we lead?

Unfortunately, I learned the hard way to answer these questions—grappling with my own issues of codependency and a deeply unhealthy soul.

My husband and I lifted a heavy ministry load as young church planters in Boston. Strategizing, supporting, and serving 24:7 as we started our family eventually took its toll on my physical health. Though I was sure of my call to ministry, my head was literally spinning under the weight of responsibilities. One thing seemed certain: God does not invite us to lead at the expense of our own soul health. The best leaders know this to be true.

I thought I had witnessed it all back then. Sadly, over the years, as we all know, the stories keep coming. Unreasonable pressure, unrealistic expectations, inauthentic exchanges, misguided egos, and off-track estimations of "success" have set up plenty of leadership meltdowns and embedded themselves in countless toxic church cultures. In the aftermath, some really good people have paid dearly. Time after time, my heart breaks watching teams fracture—shattering the faith of too many onlookers.

Imagine how the Lord feels about it all. Over-tapped, our heart, soul, mind, and strength have nothing left to pour out to Him or anyone else. If this is how you and I lead, the trickle of faith left within is endanger of drying up.

But there is a better way. Thanks to the grace of God displayed by wise spiritual directors, discerning counsel, and faithful spiritual friendships, I found my way. And so will you.

In 2012, I first crossed paths with Ed Khouri as part of a collaborative team for "The Heart and Soul Conference: Forming Spiritual and Emotional Maturity" to honor Dallas and Jane Willard. A like-minded companion on the spiritual journey, Ed's ministry exactly complements the four tenets behind Whisper Ranch: the importance of Being, Becoming, Belonging, and Blessing. These are what our souls long for and what affords the deep healing and sustainable transformation we all need during a divisive point in history.

In *The Weight of Leadership: How Codependency and Misplaced Mercy Undermine Life and Ministry,* Ed helps us examine and rebalance the load. Masterfully upending outdated leadership paradigms, he revisits grace as the basis for our attachment to God and others, as he helps readers recognize and offload unhealthy, codependent habits and relationships. Here leaders find a refreshingly practical model for how to grow healthy mercy in themselves, enjoy well-rounded personal relationships, and build grace-based teams.

The Weight of Leadership brings timely direction and hope to leaders everywhere. My prayer is that the Church of the future embraces this deeply grounded form of leadership—one immersed in silence, emotional awareness, and healthy relationships.

—**Mindy Caliguire,**
Soulcare.com
Boulder, Colorado

Acknowledgments

I write because I dream.

Deep in the gut of my life and ministry lies this dream of soul-feeding, grace-based connection with God—that each of us would know our irrevocable place as His special and favorite in a way that will change the world and our relationships within it. As leaders awaken, I envision the spread of this ever-fresh relationship with Jesus between one another.

The Lord has shown us how to make this dream a reality—providing humble yet mighty relational sustainability that is far above many of the driven, codependent models popular today. Jesus' healthy ways of connecting have incredible power to fuel our life and leadership without sucking us dry. Picture it with me. As we become like Him, our transformation holds the power to rouse the world.

TO HUNGRY LEADERS:

This book reflects my dream. It is written for you leaders who resonate but are confounded about *how* to bring the reality into your context. If you long to find healthy food for your soul and those you lead, I'm here behind the counter, ready to serve. My spirit longs to help satisfy your hunger and nourish the systems, institutions, organizations, and churches you work within. By doing so, I hope to make it easier—not harder—for seekers to discover the rich and flavorful life-loving grace of Jesus too. I am grateful that those who, out of their malnutrition, continue to ask and answer hard questions like these:

- How do I view my ministry role?
- Does grace-based connection with God show itself in my identity and how I lead others?

THE WEIGHT OF LEADERSHIP

- How has fear killed my vision or bruised my team?
- When under stress, who am I as a leader?
- In what ways am I prone to fear-based codependency in my life and leadership? (We all have them.)
- How can I manage the demands of my role in healthy ways that won't burn me out or sacrifice those I love?

If your stomach is growling for deep, honest connection between your spiritual life and leadership, I welcome you to these pages. You are among a growing fellowship of transformative pastors, leaders, and small group facilitators who, like you, are famished. Never one to disappoint, God sets a banquet table before us. Pull up a chair.

TO MY FRIENDS IN THE KITCHEN:

Part of my calling is to look at leadership systems, organizations, and outputs. Because of that, it's only natural that I regularly consider certain questions: Is this the best we can do? Are we actually creating transformative people who are bold enough to be the change others crave? Why must we recycle the same old methodologies that lead to minimal, self-centered transformation? Does this really reflect Jesus' heart?

Gratefully, the Lord has provided the help of many companions to help answer these questions—feeding my curiosity and the souls of leaders. These people have taught me to ask these questions in new ways and enriched my quest for answers. I am indebted to each and every one of them.

For many years, my wife, Maritza, has shared my dream of nurturing and empowering hungry leaders to walk fully into God's design for life. Together, we've traveled the world teaching, training, and supporting leaders and ministries. She patiently listens to me think out loud as I learn from and dissect leadership systems to understand why (or if) they work. Her wisdom and prayerful encouragement flavor this exploration.

My friend Jim Wilder walks with me closer than a brother. He encourages my dreams, tenacious curiosity, and drive to discover new ways of infusing the life of Immanuel into all life and leadership. Jim and his wife, Kitty, have supported this project from the beginning.

Without the joyful work of Amy Pierson, this book would not be a reality. Her seemingly intuitive grasp of my dreams for this project helped me prepare this manuscript and put my ideas into print. This book would not have been possible without her.

Finally, I'd like to thank the many leaders I've learned from and observed over time. These include my board of directors, the pastors and elders at New Life Church, many life group and other small group leaders I've known, and the many inspiring young leaders I've met in many nations around the world.

Introduction

I have a confession to make. I love watching silly YouTube videos when I have the time. I saw one a few minutes ago that made me both roar with laughter and pause for reflection.

A would-be cowboy convinced his friends to start recording as he walked up to a chute, released the young steer behind the gate, and attempted to wrestle it to the ground in the classic Old West style. At first, the determined steer wrestler (aka a bulldogger) grabbed the steer by the horns and dug the heels of his boots into the dirt—the rodeo was *on*! He obviously expected that the bucking and thrashing animal would drop quickly. Unfortunately for the would-be cowboy, the steer had other plans. Unimpressed by the wrestler's form, the animal fought back. It wasn't long before the steer quickly gained the upper hand (or hoof, in this case). The video ended with the cowboy getting dragged around the corral, still clinging to the horns, before finally giving up as the steer trotted away, victorious.

Leadership is like that.

How many have attempted to grab leadership "by the horns," only to find themselves thrown helplessly around the arena by an animal that is too big, too strong, and too fast for them to master? Though it is good enough to loosely "qualify" for the rodeo, a relationship with God does not provide the necessary, firm grounding to work the steer. Sure, good form and training help. (The video cowboy looked like he studied and maybe even practiced the skills needed to wrestle a bull.) But where the boots meet the arena muck, good form and training *aren't* enough to get our arms around something much heavier and more intense than expected. Like that ambitious cowboy, too many good men and women are finding themselves outweighed and overcome by leadership demands, despite the passion and enthusiasm they bring to the role.

WHAT THE DATA TELLS US ABOUT LEADERS

A 2013 report from the Barna Institute entitled "Christians on Leadership, Calling, and Career" is insightful. Apparently, 82 percent of Christian adults in America believe that the United States faces a crisis of leadership because there aren't enough leaders. However, at the same time, almost 60 percent of Christians identify themselves as leaders! Barna notes, "Christians perceive a significant leadership crisis in America caused by a distinct lack of leaders. Most feel they are leaders, but many aren't confident their leadership abilities are the most important traits in a leader. This data suggests many of them are still striving to meet even their own leadership expectations, and it means many Christians may not think of their own leadership as helping to fill the leadership gap they experience."[1]

Barna's research also shows that Christians consider integrity the most important trait for a leader, but only one-sixth of those who consider themselves leaders say that integrity is their primary leadership trait. A scant 1 percent identified humility as their own primary leadership trait!

In terms of our would-be cowboy, the data suggests that Christians believe we need more people who can wrangle the steer, but most of those who think they are leaders feel they don't have the abilities required to keep from being dragged around the ring. (Perhaps a lack of integrity convinces them and their followers that they are in fact successfully wrestling the steer and are not being dragged along?)

Maybe this explains why 76 percent of pastors say they know at least one fellow pastor whose ministry has ended due to burnout.[2] Furthermore, the Barna Group's 2017 report entitled *The State of Pastors* indicates that one-third of pastors are at risk of burnout, 43 percent are at high or medium relational risk in marriage, family, friendships, or close relationships, and 20 percent have struggled with an addiction.[3] Younger pastors are at even greater risk.[4] In a 2016 survey, U.S. Protestant pastors identified the top three pressing problems for pastors as burnout (79 percent), marital problems (78 percent), and pride (73 percent). They also noted that over half of youth pastors who use porn and one-third of senior pastors who use porn believe they are addicted.[5] Not only are leaders being thrown around—this data suggests that the steer has turned to gore them.

MY EXPERIENCE

Since I first began my journey in ministry and leadership in 1980, I've had the privilege of training men and women to lead in various ministry settings on every inhabited continent. Working with young leaders has been especially rewarding! Teaching classes and workshops for students in close to ninety nations, my wife, Maritza, and I have noticed a couple of things. Ministry bulldoggers seem to have two things in common: a passion for God and a heart to see lives touched by His love. Most are magnetic—able to articulate a compelling vision that motivates others to join them in ministry. Their personal charisma readily draws a herd of like-minded men and women who want to ride the circuit with them— transforming the planet. Committed to the Great Commission, these world changers are vibrant forces impacting the globe with the love and gospel of Jesus.

Unfortunately, I've observed another thing most of them have in common that ultimately sabotages their ability to lead, leaves members of their team disillusioned, and damages those they serve. It is unresolved internal brokenness—the kind that makes it quite difficult for them to stay securely connected with God and others as the demands of leadership inevitably grow. That is when the bull takes over. It is the point in every leader's life when hard things seem to become *too* hard. Lacking the ability to form the solid, enduring attachments with God needed to sustain them and the ability to develop and maintain deep, secure attachments with others necessary for life and ministry, this person is disconnected and on their own.

In life, we all need to surround ourselves with reliable support. Every bulldogger has a team. It consists of a good "flank man," who works the chute when the cowboy is ready, and a "hazer," a cowboy who rides alongside to keep the steer running straight. It is a group effort— they split the prize. Likewise, ministry leaders need to learn how to set up a team to help wrestle with hard things, whether issues of character or issues or circumstance. That requires learning how to build and grow relationships—not just organizations.

Without reliable, foundational connections flanking a leader, it's not possible to remain healthy. The compassion that once led a person to ministry quickly turns on them. If not dumped in the dirt, this leader will find himself or herself working harder and harder to wrangle the masses and lasso their vision, as drivenness takes the saddle. It is then such a leader is at incredibly high risk of burnout, cravings, and relational problems—all alone at the business end of the steer.

Personal charisma and vision casting, often masking deficits in relational skills with strong charisma and powerful articulation of vision, can only compensate for a lack of relational foundation for so long. The conscious and unconscious motivations behind these behaviors can keep a leader's issues cloaked—to themselves and to those in the stands. On the surface conscious and unconscious motivations can look like strengths. But as the dynamics of their internal struggles, addictions, pain, and moral failures stay hidden, the issues gain strength. The momentum moves things along until, at some point, the leader lands on his Levi's. Typically, when the dust clears, this kind of bulldogger is found bewildered and covered in it.

I read the confession of a former "rock star pastor" recently. My heart broke for the gifted and exposed young man. Responding to media reports about his failure, he stated, "When you lead out of an empty place, you make choices that have real consequences. I was unfaithful in my marriage, the most important relationship in my life, and held accountable for that."[6] Albeit too late to save himself in his position, this ex-pastor is living the consequence of exactly what I'm talking about. Running cattle alone and empty is a setup for a fall. Think about the suffering of countless others, left to their own secret devices, guilt, and unhealthy shame. Our leaders are in danger of getting gored.

COVERED IN DUST

If the leadership data and my observations from training leaders are reasonably accurate, we have an incredible problem. Let me repeat myself: we have not taught our leaders a full scope of skills that they need in order to lead well. The methods currently used to train these brave souls don't adequately prepare them for the challenges that occur once the chute opens. The weight of leadership is enormous, so we cannot afford to continue misidentifying leaders and then training them with incomplete skills. When the going gets tough, it makes for a rough ride.

So, how can Christians learn to lead relationally, boots firmly planted in the kind of grace-filled relationships that will help them sustain—and even thrive—in ministry? We need to shift the focus from knowing *about* God to knowing and being known by Him, intimately. In faith circles, you and I need to move from talking *about* community to becoming a deeply connected gathering of souls on the journey together.

Forty years of ministry have taught me that most leaders lack the kind of richly established connection with the Lord that I've described. To be clear, I am not saying that many current leaders have *no* connection with God. I'm suggesting that in many cases their relationships are not deep enough to maintain an ongoing attachment with Him under increasing stress levels. At least not for long. Likewise, the skills needed to replenish their depleted relational resources are simply inadequate for the weight of leadership. Then, when personal pain and fear outweigh their connection with God, burnout and relational failures are likely. As is true for everyone, a leader's job description includes pain and pressure occasionally. The difference is, many people expect Christian leaders to perform at a higher standard *all* the time. For the leader struggling in a hard season, a lack of transparent relationships with family, friends, and mentors just makes the burden worse.

That is not to say that if you and I are leading well, we should never feel pressured. All of us endure periods when we have to work hard and fast to serve a need or a person God has placed in our path. But if heavy pressure and a furious pace mark every day of our leadership, relational connections are often crushed under the load. Burnout warning! Cultivating a lifestyle of quieting to connect with God is essential. It makes room for the Lord to fuel our hearts for Him and the tasks He has set before us. Grounded in our connection with Him, we must make the development of healthy, relational, grace-based connections with others our priority.

For the most part, those who do not invest time in such quiet connection with the Lord or building a team aren't bad people. Most likely, they are victims of their religious environment. Where they came from, it was never modeled or taught. Taking cues from Western culture, too many Christian leaders have allowed things like personal agendas and collective angst to take hold of what belongs in God's strong hands. The subsequent load of people pleasing and performance then shifts squarely onto their shoulders—and it is a formula for failure.

And in ministry culture, it is just plain dangerous—both for the personal well-being of leaders and for the communities they lead. The mass of such misappropriation is crushing. If you are chronically overburdened, hyperextended, or hassled in your leadership role, you are probably assuming a bulk of responsibility for which you are not designed. Likewise, suppose you bear the primary burden for fulfilling an exciting vision and feel the ultimate responsibility to keep followers motivated to reach the goal; in that case, you carry a weight of leadership too heavy to bear.

LIFTING THE WEIGHT

We live the very definition of codependency when you or I carry the weight of people or things that don't belong to us. Often with good intention, we find ourselves bounding from vision to vision or need to need, offering our plans, motivation, or help. Young leaders are particularly at risk. People skills and persuasive plans eventually wane. We will wear out. Without taking time to quiet and connect with God, we can't possibly hear the directional whispers of the Holy Spirit's still small voice.

In the King James Version, Proverbs 29:18 says, "Where there is no vision, the people perish." I can't count the number of occasions I've heard this verse misquoted to explain the importance of articulating a clear and compelling vision for people to follow. Immature leaders with vibrant, personal charisma are especially at risk for misuse of this verse. Taken in context, the original word translated as *vision* refers to the kind of revelation that comes from God. The weight remains in *His* hands. It's not about motivating others to fulfill a compelling vision—it's about articulating a clear revelation coming directly from God or Scripture. To be led by God in our leadership means being purposeful to make room for Him to share His heart for us and the kinds of things He'd like us to join Him in.

This type of revelation only comes from spending time quieting with God—listening and connecting to him. Doing so promises us joy, wisdom, comfort, and direction. It is the source of vibrant, sustainable ministry. The relationship and revelation required to lead must flow from here. Without relationship and revelation, we will wear ourselves out on needs and strategies that are not God's. Like the stagger after a blindfolded spin for pin the tail on the donkey, we will struggle for our balance and bearings. Searching sightlessly for a target, we risk a fall.

Codependency is spiritually disorienting, and unchecked, it will break the best leader. Dizzied by the blur, burnout happens when the misplaced weight of what we are carrying exceeds our capacity to stay connected with God and others. Before long, replenishment becomes difficult, if not impossible. The result is a deficit in our souls. Adversely affected, our emotional and mental health is damaged, impacting relationships and increasing a sense of distance from God. After a while, hopelessness and despair slink into our thought life. Soon, the bottom drops out. It is a set up for depression and exhaustion as our coping strategies turn to addictions. Our joy gets hijacked. Things that bring worldly thrills or false peace vie for the affection that rightly belongs to God.

To express this vision of vibrant, grace-based leadership and to help you keep codependency at bay, these pages will guide you to explore the following:

- a more complete understanding of grace
- the fear factor
- the poison of codependency
- mercy as a posture
- the antidote
- values of grace-based leadership
- the necessary relational shift, and
- putting it all together

Needless to say, the damage of codependency and burnout don't just strike those in pastoral roles. Navigating life with God and other people is tricky in all walks of life. The best leadership traits in the world won't keep you out of the manure. Keeping awe, respect, and firm grace-based connections with the Lord and others as our foundation, we quickly find that good learning alone leads us nowhere. Nobody wants to land there. So, "cowboy up," and learn how God longs to meet you in lasting, life-changing ways that will empower your leadership . . . otherwise, the bull wins.

1 *Airports and Pie*

> *"I have been crucified with Christ; it is no longer I who live, but Christ lives in me; and the life which I now live in the flesh I live by faith in the Son of God, who loved me and gave Himself for me. I do not set aside the grace of God; for if righteousness comes through the law, then Christ died in vain."*

—GALATIANS 2:20–21

> *Little Jack Horner*
> *Sat in the corner,*
> *Eating a Christmas pie;*
> *He put in his thumb,*
> *And pulled out a plum,*
> *And said, "What a good boy am I!"*

—"LITTLE JACK HORNER" BY MOTHER GOOSE

Some things just don't make sense. Here is just a sampling of what popped up recently when I queried Google for "things that don't make sense." Consider these quandaries for a second:

- Why do we call our planet Earth when it is mostly water?
- Why are pizza boxes square?
- Why don't cartoon characters ever change their clothes?
- Why is there no ham in a hamburger?
- Why do we think Baby Yoda is so cute?

(Okay. I admit it. That last one is mine.)

Grace should be on that list. It doesn't make sense, after all, but that is just the way it is.

Like gravity, grace seems to go against reason. Thankfully, however, it is the way it is. According to His grace, God deems you and me "special and favorite." Much more than just an "unmerited gift," grace is God extending a warm relationship to each of us. And we have the opportunity—the command, really—to lovingly reach out to one another the same way.

Many of us know what that looks like. We are all the same in this ability: just like yours, my body can tell when someone is glad to be with me. It experiences a high-energy neurological response called joy. Literally, *my* brain can see their eyes sparkle—a sign that dopamine has been released in *their* brain. Before I consciously know what is happening, the joy bringer's body language has made their inviting dopamine mark on my brain too.

Think of grace as the gift of an ongoing state of reunion—we turn toward God to find Him ever eagerly awaiting our company. Still unclear on what grace is? Think of people reuniting at the airport. There is a certain expectancy. In our airport there is a passenger waiting area. At any given time people cluster just at the base of the escalators holding Welcome Home signs, smiling broadly, fidgeting with heightened anticipation, and straining to see the one they love emerge from the secured area of the concourse. When their eyes meet, there is an undeniable exchange of energy, tears—JOY!—at finally being together again. Awareness of all others melts away as the special and favorite traveler emerges from the crowd. Hearty bear hugs ensue, along with happy tears. Faces light up with *Welcome Home*! Clearly, this is where we all belong—or what we long for. While the giddiness of reunion eventually settles into a more peaceful state, the pleasure of being close to the special one remains. Glad to be together, this is the embodiment of God's heart of grace toward us. As we travel along our spiritual journey, the question is, *Will you and I search for Him in the waiting area or head straight to claim our baggage?*

IMAGINE THE TIME APART

If you have dear ones that live far away, you more than understand. When they are near, your connection with these special people brings a certain wholeness to your being. They are part of who you are. When you part, something is missing. To be unconditionally received and welcomed and delighted in is a gift God gives us. It is ours to respond—to keep our hearts ever turned toward Him. Baggage doesn't matter.

To fully receive such absolute acceptance and warmth trains you and me to recognize a "face of grace" before us; that is, I can tell that this delightful other person sees me as special and favorite. The lovingkindness of grace refreshes us as weary travelers. Whether we know to look for it or not, we are drawn back to it, again and again. In each of our lives, joy greets us to express grace, and grace expresses joy in a reciprocal fashion. Where you and I find one, we always find the other. Whether internally or externally, when my brain's pleasure center recognizes joy, it flashes back a look of grace-filled light. That grace, in turn, releases a surge of dopamine in the joy carrier's body. It's science. Grace and joy travel together, creating the strongest relational bonds possible.

Such bonds are essential for good leadership. In a disconnected and lonely world, grace is exactly what so many are looking for—and it is not something you can fake. Authentically demonstrating to people that they are special and favorite is far more life-changing than any theories about grace that you or I could espouse. Those who learn to genuinely welcome and interact with that same "welcome home warmth" of belonging toward others will notice how far it goes to help people actually experience it. If you want to be a great leader, learn to model grace. It will empower everything you do . . . and it's actually quite sweet.

SWEET (AND SAVORY) AS THE WHOLE PIE

Grace is like pie. It just says, "Welcome!" There is just something comforting and wholesome about it. Baking pie well is both art and science—it's very trendy these days too. But pie has a history. Word has it that the Greeks and Romans ate it. According to those who know, the Greeks favored meat pies (think shepherd's pie, chicken pot pie, empanadas, samosas, runzas, etc.), while Romans enjoyed theirs sweet (of the fruit variety, often served as dessert).[7] Do you suppose Jesus had a favorite? Would he have liked sweet or savory? (If I didn't know better, I'd say I'm Roman.)

Like pie, grace is nothing new. As you and I snarf down a serving, few of us consider what has gone into it. More historical pie facts: pie crust is not just tasty; back in the day, it was also functional as a baking dish and storage container. It helped preserve the flavorful contents, be they fruit or meat. Depending on our taste or appetite, you and I can get a little too finicky about the parts of grace we like. For instance, we want salvation but can do without forgiving the guy who cut us off in traffic. Instead of enjoying the whole, we pick out our favorite parts—the fruit, the sugar-washed crust, or such—and barely touch all the rest that there is to enjoy.

It sounds like Little Jack Horner was much like us. Well-informed legend has it that his story is far more than a children's nursery rhyme. The verse serves up a slice of significant church history. Throughout his English kingdom in the late 1530s, Henry VIII was dissolving monasteries and stealing land from the Catholic Church. Sensing the religious climate change, Richard Whiting knew something must be done. As the abbot of Glastonbury (one such endangered English monastery), he cooked up a plan to curry the king's erratic favor. Abbot Whiting would offer King Henry twelve smaller "plum" properties in hopes of preserving his beloved monastery.

As apparently happened in those days, the deeds were secretly baked into a pie and delivered to London by the abbot's steward, one Thomas Horner—aka Jack. Either Jack got hungry along the way or pure greed overcame him. Whatever the case, clever Jack's piece contained the deed for Mells Manor, a beautiful estate that remained in the Horner family for generations after that day. Eventually, the remaining pie and eleven other deeds were received at the palace. Sadly, in the end Glastonbury Abbey was still seized along with its treasures, and the abbot was imprisoned in the Tower of London and ultimately put to death.

SETTLING FOR A SLICE

History notwithstanding, I like pie. A lot. All kinds actually. Peach, key lime, pumpkin, pecan—whatever—I'll take it. I have a hankering for the sweet variety, as you can tell. Warm or cold, I love the flavor bomb of fruit and flaky pastry crust. When someone brings pie over to our house, I want *all* the deliciousness—not just one plum . . . not even just one slice! If there are leftovers, I will enjoy a good pie for days—savoring every morsel. Admittedly, I'm not satisfied until the pie plate is clean. I may not want to eat it all at once, but when I have a hunger for more, it is good to know that the pantry is not bare.

Think about your favorite pie. When someone brings you a pie and serves you a piece, do you pick at the plums? Do you take just one piece and throw the rest away? Grace is like pie. Taking just one little bit of it (like the popular part that relates to salvation or God's unconditional love) is good, but there is so much more to enjoy! I fear far too many

Christians aren't into grace for the whole relational pie. They only eat the parts they like. The rest gets tossed. This makes grace a product and them persnickety consumers. Like Little Jack Horner, they just want a plum or two that a slice of God's grace provides. Taking grace for what's in it for them, they pick at certain pieces and leave the rest on their plate.

UNSATISFYING

If that is your view of grace, trust me, at some point in life you will find yourself spiritually unsatisfied. Missing the best parts of it, you'll either push back from the table stuffed but disappointed, or you'll go in search of something else more pleasing to your personal taste. That is probably because what religion has served up for you has been missing something up to this point. So you don't waste away, it is time to consider how the spiritual limits of stuffy and starved grace teachings have left us unnecessarily hungry. Underfed, this doesn't just leave the body of Christ famished, but it diminishes our love and enjoyment of the whole.

OUR EXTRAVAGANT HOLY HOST

God is an extravagant host. When He serves His special and favorite ones dessert, God invites each of us to enjoy an *entire* pie. He won't force-feed us, but it's there. With every bite, this lavish offering is meant to guide us—full, loving, and satisfied—to the One we love most. What is served from His kitchen is baked with delicious, grace-based ingredients for the wholeness of our unique biblical identity. At His table, by his grace, we discover the full flavor of who we *truly* are.

More than a theological piece of the pie, the salvation grace offers is meant to be an invitation to an ongoing relationship with God—the Holy Host at the head of the table. And we are meant to share a taste of it with others. Though it *can* be scripturally supported, the filling of grace isn't made of data, dogma, or head knowledge. Grace takes the form of an intentional, ongoing relationship. So would you like some pie—the *whole* grace pie and all its pieces? Most certainly, the relational flavor it will add to your life with God and others will make you come back for more, again and again. Seeing and being seen through eyes of grace always brings us back!

"Therefore, from now on, we regard no one according to the flesh. Even though we have known Christ according to the flesh, yet now we know Him thus no longer. Therefore, if anyone is in Christ, he is a new creation; old things have passed away; behold, all things have become new" (2 Corinthians 5:16–17).

GRACE-FILLED ATTACHMENT: MAGNETS AND MIRRORS

Attachment is what God envisions for us. You and I have been created for a life of connection with Him and among one another. As Creator, He knows that our closest relational connections have the greatest impact on our behavior. Psychologists call these close, powerful relationships that endure over time "attachments," and we begin making them the moment we are born (some even hypothesize attachment begins in the womb). For better or worse, attachments shape the parts of our lives that determine the development of a healthy brain and central nervous system as well as a solid identity and personality.

Attachment based on grace—knowing ourselves as unconditionally special and favorite to another—creates a force that is hard to resist. Our souls are like magnets to the steel of it. Above anything else, who you or I love will draw and determine how we behave. Those we attach to are our "mirrors," reflecting back our value and worth through repeated interactions. From the start, healthy relationships with our primary caregivers help us to see ourselves as valuable, loveable, worthwhile people who are capable of bringing others joy. If I experience myself as deeply beloved like this to another, it isn't hard to understand why grace-based, relational attachment is far more important to my discipleship than what

I *know*. God and His grace are designed to be our primary "guidance system."

NOTHING TO BE AFRAID OF

Only one kind of righteous fear crosses paths with healthy, grace-based attachment. The sole form of fear that God finds acceptable comes from the Greek word *eulábeia*. Godly *eulábeia* translates as "devout or fearful devotion" to define an internal attitude of reverence toward a person, thing, or event. Hebrews 12:28 furthers our understanding: "Therefore, since we are receiving a kingdom which cannot be shaken, let us have grace, by which we may serve God acceptably with reverence and godly fear." As God's people, it is right for us to be fearfully devoted to Him in this way. Connected and aware of His lovingkindness, you and I will naturally follow Him with a sense of honor, awe, love, and respect. God's Word and relationship light a path ahead. Beyond fearful devotion to God in our lives, fear and grace part ways here.

GUIDANCE AS A GAME SHOW

Kind of like the game show *Let's Make a Deal*, we all have a choice to take or trade what God has freely offered us. We make our deals on the daily stage.

- Deal #1: God's Grace-Based Guidance (This one is a winner!)—A priceless and reliable prize, dependent on God and the guidance He offers us through secure, grace-based attachment, or
- Deal #2: Self's Fear-Based Guidance (Here you have an overrated "zonk," *Let's Make a Deal* lingo for a booby prize!)—This leaves us alone, reliant on self-guidance, and tapping our own resources.

Obviously, grace-based guidance (Deal #1) is God's best for us. But aside from the name, why should the fear-based guidance of self not be what we want to take home? Simply put, it is not trustworthy. Disconnected from rather than being guided by grace, choosing what is behind this curtain still leaves you and me on our own, longing to feel special and favorite in the world. We opt for this out of fear, deciding to see what we can work out alone. Usually, we do it in all the wrong ways. That's because it is not easy to navigate life by our individual opinions of what is right and what is wrong. Make no mistake, Satan loves it when we venture out on our own believing we're making good choices. As you may well imagine, once we start doing things our own way, he throws a few more temptations to keep us playing the game . . . and losing.

When we play this way, before long you and I have left God's grace behind without realizing it. Making fear-based decision after fear-based decision, we find self-guidance has led us far from the true prize of God and His grace. Paul spelled it out for the Galatians: "I suspect you would never intend this, but this is what happens. When you attempt to live by your own religious plans and projects, you are cut off from Christ, you fall out of grace. Meanwhile we expectantly wait for a satisfying relationship with the Spirit. For in Christ, neither our most conscientious religion nor disregard of religion amounts to anything. What matters is something far more interior: faith expressed in love" (Galatians 5:4–6 MSG).

So, each of us has a unique choice to make: 1) Will I continue to interact with God in each moment—engaging with Him to discover the full riches of our relationship and enjoy His grace-based guidance, or 2) will I opt for the guidance of self and my own resources—disconnecting from God as I go? Fear heads off under the darkened direction of self, while grace chooses a more glorious path.

FALLING FAR FAST

Back to the beginning for a minute. Attachment based on God's grace is the direction we need for life. Adam and Eve are a classic example of two people who started in grace but wandered into self and fear as their guidance system. They were the first contestants (however, truth be told, they didn't *have* to play in order to win). God set Adam and Eve in the garden knowing exactly how capable they were.

Though I'm sure the happy couple had much to learn from their Father, things seemed to be going pretty well there for a while. That is, until they recognized their own resourcefulness and got a little too big for their fig leaves. Disregarding God's direction, Adam and Eve's decision to eat what was off-limits knocked perfection on its heels.

With our newfound understanding about grace and attachment, in hindsight it is so easy to judge their foolishness, isn't it? Yet on any given day you and I are prone to the same bad choices. Given our resourceful and capable nature, we can run far afield before we realize we are not in the garden under God's gracious direction anymore. Doing things all on our own, we end up reaping what we've sown—with handfuls of thistles thrown in.

Many have followed the way Adam and Eve led for us. Instead of trusting their position as God's favorites, they decide to try to make themselves more special by relying on their own resources. As leaders, when we trust in our own capabilities as a guidance system, it will always end badly. Not only does it tend to destroy our lives and ministries, but our example will also lead those who follow us astray.

Still, God invites us back.

WEAKNESS AS A REQUIREMENT

Knowing our weaknesses and proclivity to wander from His way, the Lord boldly reassures you and me as He did Peter, "My grace is sufficient for you, for My strength is made perfect in weakness" (2 Corinthians 12:9). You see, God's grace is a *direct* response to our weakness. When we say yes and attach to His grace, something in you and me is acknowledging, "I am weak and it is okay . . . because He is not."

Have we forgotten?

It is so important that you and I remember the place in grace that Jesus died to give us. By His very nature, grace is a "we" thing. No more lone ranger, white-knuckle religious wrangling. James 4:6 couldn't be more clear: "God resists the proud, but gives grace to the humble." Stop there. Step back and take a long slow look. Peering more closely into the original Greek, the word *proud* comes from a compound word and means "to overshine." In other words, anytime that we try to shine brighter than those around us, and/or trust our own resources more than God, we can bet we have missed grace. Hogging the spotlight is never a good idea.

Does the mirror of God's Word reflect your life here? Look closer. Can you see the hope of change coming? Engaging with God to discover His grace will change your attachment with Him forever. It will shift the light of glory back to God where it belongs, too, and little by little, life by life, embracing grace this way will change the face of the Christian church! Connected to God in a loving relationship, you and I will love and keep on loving His commandments (John 14:15). We will love our neighbors as ourselves—living responsively together in His interactive presence. We will stay engaged, not aloof; compassionate, not critical. All of a sudden, this life will become an ongoing exchange among dearest friends. Things will be as God intended all along. In the words of Dallas Willard, you and I are meant to live in close community wherein the "primary Sustainer" of our friendships is its "most glorious inhabitant."[8] Despite our limitations, He adores us as we do Him. In fact, He can't get enough of us.

So welcome home! Now go get yourself some pie.

2 *Fear and Codependency*

Do you see what we've got? An unshakable kingdom! And do you see how thankful we must be? Not only thankful, but brimming with worship, deeply reverent before God. For God is not an indifferent bystander. He's actively cleaning house, torching all that needs to burn, and he won't quit until it's all cleansed. God himself is Fire!

—HEBREWS 12:28–29 MSG

I must not fear. Fear is the mind-killer. Fear is the little-death that brings total obliteration. I will face my fear.

—FRANK HERBERT, *DUNE*

If we were to understand how dear we are to God, our relation to Him, our value in His eyes, and how He protects us by His faithful promises and gracious presence, we would not tremble at every appearance of danger.

—JOHN FLAVEL, *TRIUMPHING OVER SINFUL FEAR*

There I stood in Walmart. I was making a regular grocery run after returning from a long trip. As I rounded the end-aisle display heading for the paper goods and cleaning supplies, it came into view: fifty feet of completely empty shelf space. The shelves were totally stripped—top to bottom. *What happened to all the toilet paper?* I wondered. I was looking around for someone "official" to ask where all the toilet paper went when I noticed carts crowding the unusually long checkout lines. After a couple more beats, my attention was drawn to the number of carts in those lines that were crammed to the brim with canned goods, bottled water, and all the twelve-packs of bath tissue and paper towels each cart could hold. *Did I miss a hurricane warning?*

Now, I don't pretend to understand the personal needs of my fellow shoppers, but something about the panic purchase of all these rolls struck me as humorous . . . at first, that is. My mood quickly sobered, however, as I realized the fear that was driving the frenzy. A global pandemic had newly gripped our part of the globe, restrooms first. Hoping to make it through, these folks were stockpiling personal reserves!

That is the way fear is: when you and I fall prey, our first reaction is to clutch and control whatever we can to stay alive—or at least end up in a better position than the next guy. Panicked and doing our best to survive with our own stash of resources, we self-protect and hoard what we think we need. Even among the best of us, our Christian values are far too easily jettisoned at this point in a crisis. We may even rationalize, "It's the responsible thing to do," as we simultaneously give no thought to anyone else. But trust me, putting faith in what *you* can see and what makes *you* comfortable in order to mediate fear never works very well for long. That's because all the toilet paper and survival skills we can muster have nothing to do with God's primary guidance system for our lives.

God's guidance system is grace-based attachment. It is a magnetic and powerful connection with Him that will decide our destiny if we let it. But if grace does not capture our hearts, there is another system—

fear-based guidance—that ever vies for the power and control of our hearts and minds.

STORM WARNING

Fear-based guidance systems suck us in—often innocently, logical-ly, reactively—as we "handle things" that come up by ourselves. Look-ing again at Scripture, you can see the warning signs. The clouds that gathered over the thoughts and motives of Adam and Eve still loom on the horizon of our own. Once God pointed out the good and tasty fruit on the tree and told them that they weren't allowed to touch, do you suppose they began to wonder if they could do better? Could they make themselves more special and favorite with just a bite? Was God holding out on them? Whatever the case, Eve wanted it. One day, that want turned to need—a need she decided to try to meet on her own apart from God. Fully aware of what *he* was doing, Adam chose the fruit and his wife over his relationship with God. We all know how the story of their disconnection goes from there.

Once detached, their death spiral began—a fear-nado twisting their attention and attachment to themselves. Then, in the aftermath, stripped of all they'd been given, the two realized their selfish mistake. And when they did, God's favorite human companions raced into the jungle tearing at limbs and leaves to cover their weaknesses. The Father found them hiding beneath the debris of their self-guided decision and gently called them out. (Sound familiar?)

A MEALY MOUTHFUL

Scripture tells us Eden's trees were "pleasing to the eye and good for food" (Genesis 2:9 NIV). A far cry from the stinking rot of death. Think-ing about Adam and Eve taking a bite of that clearly forbidden fruit, I can't help but imagine the (dis)taste they were left with. No doubt Eve took the fruit believing it would make her *more* special and favorite than she already was. (Impossible!) The initial sweetness of the produce must have quickly given way to a unripened and mealy reality. Fooled by its pleasant appearance and tasty reputation, Eve unwittingly initiated an introduction to the bitterness of sin and death. As soon as Adam bit into the fruit, did they see the worms that suddenly appeared—wriggling in the flesh of their unholy harvest? (I've got a CGI in my head morphing the perfect piece of fruit to rancid remains.) Second-guessing God's good way, thinking they wanted something more, the two consumed what wasn't meant for them—changing God's perfection into something putrid. They swallowed every parasitic mouthful of it. At once, their eyes were opened. The consequence poisoned what had been a joyful life with God and was digested to become part of our human nature—it processed and absorbed in the form of fear and separation for us all. The future of relationships forever corrupted. Recognize: this was the first time they felt the need to hide.

Blech! Doesn't it make you sick?!

TURNING GOD'S STOMACH

If you have ever regretted a big mistake or raised adult children you've watched suffer through consequences of bad decisions, you can imagine how it turned God's compassionate stomach. With one presumptuous bite, you and I were separated from grace—our position as His special and favorite. Instead, our corrupted fleshly nature has been reset to a default of fear. Apart from grace, doubt and dread replace peace and joy.

Now, let's think of this in terms of leadership. If we miss it, the implications are dire. Each time you and I succumb to the temptation to turn our own way—putting confidence in ourselves and whatever resources or solutions we can scrounge up—we've taken a mealy mouthful of this nasty fruit. We've strayed from our relationship with God, detached from His guidance, and moved our own direction . . . *and we are taking others with us.* Convinced by the adequacy of self and our own resources, you and I separate from God with a foolish sense that we can rightly decide what to do and where to go in our lives and leading. Then, when things don't turn out as we planned, we find ourselves ambushed by fear—ashamed, afraid, and often feeling exposed. It is, after all, our default. Alone in a crowd, this is a shrewdly-laid trap for God's capable leaders.

BAD SEED

Does this sound like God's fault? No. The fear-laden seeds of this bad orchard are sown by the father of lies, not the God of Grace. God is love—patient, kind, rejoicing when truth wakes us up. He consistently protects, trusts, hopes, and always perseveres in demonstrating that we are his special and favorite ones (1 Corinthians 13:4–6). He has no illusions about who we are or how we are being—or have been—guided and formed.

There are three different Greek words used for fear in the New Testament. What made Adam and Eve ready to run from the garden was not godly fear, awe, and reverential respect (the definition of the Greek word *eulabela*, mentioned in the previous chapter). It was one of the other two words used in the New Testament. The first we will consider is *phobos* or *phobeo*. For its specific meaning in context is important, as you will see. The second word is *deiliao*. And we will look at it separately.

PHOBOS/PHOBEO ≈ FEAR

First, *phobos* or *phobeo*. Sometimes this word is used to express a reverential fear of the Lord, which is an entirely appropriate response to the majesty and infinite grace of God. This is the kind of awe-inspired fear Moses displayed when he fell on his face before the Lord. A healthy sense of phobeo is also conveyed throughout Luke 12:4–7 (NIV): "I tell you, my friends, do not be afraid of those who kill the body and after that can do no more. But I will show you whom you should fear: fear him who, after your body has been killed, has authority to throw you into hell. Yes, I tell you, fear him. Are not five sparrows sold for two pennies? Yet not one of them is forgotten by God. Indeed, the very hairs of your head are all numbered. Don't be afraid; you are worth more than many sparrows." Ephesians 5:21 further demonstrates a similar application of the word: this is the kind of fear (phobos) that God endorses and is entirely reasonable.

Another, less positive context for the word *phobeo* is also found in Scripture. The distinct definition of this kind of fear is the one that made Adam and Eve run. It translates as terror. God does not want His people to operate in fear of this variety. For example, Romans 8:14–15 (NIV) reads, "For those who are led by the Spirit of God are the children of God. The Spirit you received does not make you slaves, so that you live in fear again; rather, the Spirit you received brought about your adoption to sonship. And by him we cry, 'Abba, Father.'" Clearly, here we can see that this kind of fear is antithetical to God's heart and the gifts He gives to His people.

Thankfully, God has an antidote for the virus of fear and its fruits, terror and punishment. (Pay attention, toilet paper hoarders.) First John 4:18–19 helps expand our understanding: "And we have known and believed the love that God has for us. God is love, and he who abides in love abides in God, and God in him. Love has been perfected [*teleióo*: complete, mature] among us in this: that we may have boldness in the day of judgment; because as He is, so are we in this world. There is no fear [phobos] in love; but perfect love casts out fear, because fear involves torment [*kólasis*: torment, punishment]. But he who fears has not been made perfect in love. We love Him because He first loved us." It's not just God's love, presence, and grace that displace fear—it is also the presence of others with a more mature and perfected love.

God's presence grows us out of fear into maturity. He provides the grace-based guidance system we need for life and leadership. Unless or until God removes the reality of fear and torment, it is where you and I will naturally live. This kind of fear promises to hold us captive, stunt our growth, and stress us out. Jesus wants to drive this kind of fear out of our lives and has sent the Holy Spirit (His presence) to continue the process of helping us grow fully into the freedom of God's sons and daughters.

DEILIAO ≈ FEAR

Now onto the second commonly used New Testament word for fear: the Greek word *deiliao*. It denotes a timidity or cowardice that is never befitting God's people. A look at 2 Timothy 1:7 clarifies its proper meaning: "For God has not given us a spirit of fear, but of power and of love and of a sound mind."

Anytime we accommodate a spirit of either deiliao or phobos in our leadership, you and I usher fear in the door . . . and it will make a wreck of the place with the terror, torment, and punishment it packs. When these arrive, they always multiply. Quietly and casually, our faith shifts from God's grace to our own capacity and abilities. At the very least, we must call it a compromise. Because fear often makes a sneaky entrance, here are some common, subconscious beliefs that may be undermining your life and ministry:

- I will not have the approval of the people I seek it from.
- I will not perform well enough or "measure up."
- I will fail.
- People will accuse me of being a bad Christian.
- I will be rejected or lose a relationship or position that is valuable.
- I will not have enough.
- I will feel ashamed.

- People will say bad things about me.
- People won't make it without me.
- I'm not sure what God's saying, but I need to make a decision anyway.
- When in doubt, my gifting will get me through.
- My own resources or the resources of my church or ministry will take care of things.

FEAR IS OUR DEFAULT SYSTEM

Most of us who use tablets or smartphones are familiar with the term *default system*. Samsung products come preloaded with an Android operating system as its default, while Apple's default operating system is iOS. Both govern the way we use our devices—dictating its capabilities and limits. Whatever our operating system, you and I get so used to how it works that the idea of switching is practically inconceivable.

As part of our nature, you and I are also "preloaded" with a default operating system that guides both our spiritual life and our central nervous system—that guidance system is fear.

Spiritually speaking, Scripture spells it out: "Since the children are made of flesh and blood, it's logical that the Savior took on flesh and blood in order to rescue them by his death. By embracing death, taking it into himself, he destroyed the Devil's hold on death and freed all who cower through life, scared to death of death" (Hebrews 2:14–15 MSG). Until we respond to God's graceful gift of salvation, fear of death—and the accompanying torment and terror—are our default system for life. It is removed only as our grace-based attachment with God grows and matures throughout our lifetime.

Our nervous system works the same way. You and I enter the world unattached to anyone or anything—physically and psychologically—born of Adam, born into fear. From birth, our brain's alarm system in the relational center of the brain is on alert. This system works to protect us from danger, and spurs us to fight, flight, or freeze in order to survive. From day one, our brain is committed to keeping us safe. Fear is our nervous system's default setting, and to learn to operate effectively, our fear and alarm center needs calibration. It must learn that not every new situation is a threat and not every person is scary. In a world full of potentially scary encounters, it needs training in order to work right—only sounding the alarm for genuine threats.

What helps train this alarm/stress center for life? The answer is simple. In our early years, our brain learns to function appropriately by experiencing strong, consistent grace-based interactions with Mom, Dad, and other primary caregivers. These grace-rich, joy-empowered interactions teach our alarm/stress centers that the world is not always a bad and scary place. The stronger our grace-based attachments grow, the better our alarm center functions. Our nervous system actually learns and practices a new, more peaceful default system for life: grace.

Without such early training to establish a solid grace-based foundation, our body's stress and alarm systems become malformed and will fail. A fire alarm is a fine thing to have in place in the event of an actual fire, but do you remember when you were in school, and someone pulled the fire alarm or it inexplicably went on the fritz? The wail and whoop of its obnoxious tone was loud and startling and caused an abrupt interruption of all activity. The prank made it impossible to concentrate on anything.

That is what it's like for our central nervous system when stress sets off its alarm unnecessarily. For some more often than others, something inside "pulls the fire alarm," and the incessant internal blaring begins. Despite no actual fire, the pressure persists to preoccupy our system— driving reactions of fight, flight, or freeze. Needless to say, it's hard to form secure attachments and a stable identity when all we can hear is the brain-rattling bawl of such false alarms.

Throughout life, when bad things happen, the first thing our system wants to know is *Am I alone in this?* The more alone we feel, the louder our internal siren sounds. This is especially true if we have experienced early abuse or neglect in our lives. As my friend Dr. Jim Wilder has been known to say, "We are all looking for someone looking for us." The presence of such a caring other reminds us in fact that we are not on our own when bad things occur. All will be well.

Only secure, grace-based relational attachment can disarm our alarm center—teaching our system how to stand down and effectively regulate itself. When you and I are young, each time our needs for food, basic needs, and comfort are met, we learn how to do this.

Because fear is a basic foundation of *everyone's* brain structure, and since perfect parents and unicorns only exist in our dreams, each of us learns to accommodate it to varying degrees. We *all* learn to hide our fears and insecurities well enough, apart from God's grace and other people. High-functioning people—like most of those in leadership—may appear not to act out of fear when in reality they have simply learned how to hide it better than the rest of us.

THE 4 DEADLY PS: FEAR-BASED MOTIVATIONS AND BEHAVIORS THAT NUMB THEM

As we've covered, when you and I *don't* feel secure and *don't* know that we are special and favorite in the eyes of our caregiver, our default reaction is fear. Without grace, fear dominates us early. This is indicative of the deep soul-longing we each carry as a result of the inconsistent, missing, or weak grace-based attachment that we have experienced. Unchecked, the strength of these longings will continue to shape who we are and how we behave, both positively and negatively, throughout our lives.

By the time you and I are about two and a half years old, our brain has latched on to certain motivations as substitutes for the grace-based attachment that we are really after. These motivations are planted and take root deep in our subconscious mind before we're even able to talk. I call these motivations the 4 Deadly Ps. Each encompasses an unconscious way you and I may uniquely try to compensate for the secure grace that is missing—thereby soothing ourselves and settling our fears:

- **Pleasing**—Leaning on the approval of others
- **Performing**—Doing things well in the eyes of others
- **Pain Avoidance**—Avoiding what feels bad to me
- **Pleasure Seeking**—Pursuing what feels good to me

If our search for such grace and attachment moves us *away* from God and His guidance, it is just moving toward worldly, self-guided ways to help mask what we are missing. Each motivation is a flimsy disguise for fear that keeps us separated from God. When our identities are shaped more by the 4 Deadly Ps than by the graceful awareness of our relationship with God, you and I become unstable to ourselves, the groups we are part of (including our families), and those we lead.

DISCONNECTED DARLA

I recently heard about Darla, a young mother of twins. Despite all the research that is out there about the dangers of smoking while pregnant and the negative effects of secondhand smoke, Darla has continued to puff away—particularly when nursing. Because of his job in sales, her husband is on the road a lot. Needless to say, that puts her under a considerable amount of pressure. Apparently, it is not something Darla weathers very well. The nurturing opportunity to bond with her babies while breastfeeding is blown away with each drag on her cigarette.

For these infants, even though Mom is in the room, she is emotionally unavailable, distant, missing her husband, and preoccupied with the stress relief that smoking provides. The best thing about the time for each of the twins is their mother's milk. In this way, food becomes far more pleasurable than connection with Mom. At other times, when one of the babies cries, needs a diaper change, or otherwise fusses for comfort, Mom's frustration teaches them to please and perform. Though it is never spoken, these babies are learning that making their mother happy is more important than any need they may have. Sadly, the more these interactions repeat themselves, the more strongly the motivations and behaviors are reinforced in their little psyches. See how insidiously we pick up a sense of our value? From our earliest encounters, we long to see that we are special and favorite in the eyes of another. It guides us.

If not following the lead of grace-based guidance, you and I can be sure that our life is accommodating the Deadly 4 Ps. People who have strong, grace-based relationships, especially early in life, struggle far less with them. But under the influence of the 4 Deadly Ps, instead of remembering that you and I are God's special and favorite, we will find ourselves asking questions like these:

- Who do I need to please?
- Who do I need to like me so that I feel good about myself?
- How well do I have to do so I don't feel worthless?
- What can I do to make it stop?

Not one of us will find sustainable value here. Especially if you are striving to answer these life questions as a leader, you should know that living according to the 4 Deadly Ps can lead to ministry breakdown, team tension, personal burnout—and worse!

BEEPS, BEEPS!

Fear would love to steer us down this road as a way of life—taking you and me the wrong way on the spiritual freeway. (Hear the honking?) As we drive hard and fast in misguided, fear-based efforts, a crash is guaranteed as we desperately try to earn for ourselves what God has already provided. When you or I grip the wheel so tightly—latching on to the misplaced motivations surrounding the 4 Deadly Ps—we soon find ourselves dependent upon (dare I say, addicted to) Behaviors, Events, Experiences, People, and Substances (BEEPS).

BEEPS are the things you and I "use" to numb fear and pain so that life will appear to be working. The more we use BEEPS, the more powerfully they will hijack our neuropathways—affecting our mood, emotions, thinking, and levels of pain. Though they are no substitute for true grace-based attachment, these sly seconds are effective at temporarily keeping our anxieties and pain at bay. Confused? Let me introduce you to Paul.

PAUL'S STORY AND THE 4 DEADLY PS

Paul is a painful picture of the destructive power of the 4 Deadly Ps and BEEPS. He was a good kid who grew up in a very dysfunctional, alcoholic family. His dad was the drunk, but when he was sober, Paul's father seemed to really care. He let Paul know that he was special, spending time with him on fishing trips, at ball games, or over a hamburger once in a while. When he was drinking, however, his dad made everyone in the house pay for it. Yelling and physical abuse were pretty routine.

Through those years, Paul's mom spent most of her time just trying to survive and take care of the kids. Although she did her best, she wasn't emotionally available for Paul and his sisters. Understandably, her anxiety and fear about Paul's dad kept her preoccupied. The combination of both subtle and overt early life experiences led Paul to see life as a pretty scary place—one devoid of sustained grace and comfort. Needless to say, he did not feel like he was anyone's favorite or very special in the grand scheme of things. From his environment, Paul learned that if he could keep people happy at home and perform well enough to avoid upsetting people, he could avoid being singled out for punishment. (Notice two out of the 4 Deadly Ps there?)

In those years, Paul also learned that other things—like food—felt a whole lot more satisfying than trying to connect with his mom or dad. Fear of painful punishment began to drive his behaviors—especially once he entered high school. As a teen, Paul readily fell into the usage of BEEPS. He learned that alcohol could "take the edge off," marijuana made him forget, and cocaine could give him the boldness and energy he'd always wanted in order to engage with life. Instead of fear, no matter what the drug of choice, Paul found the artificial means to feel accepted, perform better, and numb awareness of his painful inadequacy. Finally, he felt "good."

Eventually, though, the use of BEEPS caught up to him. Arrests, jail time, and occasional trips to rehab came to define his life. Paul's drive to numb his loneliness and feelings of inadequacy heaped atop the memory of how his drugs made him feel—leading straight back to jail. Inevitably, vowing to do better, Paul would cycle through rehabs and support groups until his pain and memory of drug usage led him back to the beginning of the cycle. Remarkably, it is much easier for the brain to remember how good the initial high felt while tending to forget the pain that inevitably results when the cycle runs its course. His brain had been hijacked.

Finally, Paul landed in a Christian rehab program where he discovered and experienced God's love and a supportive community. Truly treated as special and favorite, he thrived! Paul began to hope for a different kind of future and worked hard to make it possible. The approval and encouragement that he got from peers and counselors paid off. Paul even began to think of helping others coming from similar situations.

Cue the next life scene: wanting to give back, Paul completed his training as an addiction counselor, found a loving wife, had several children, and began to lead his own rehab program. On the outside, he appeared to be the picture of success. A proverbial poster child, Paul led his ministry well and had a strong, supportive staff. He did his best to care for those God sent to them for help. What Paul didn't realize was that his need to be accepted and perform well was still at the wheel. It wasn't long before his drive to keep his staff and clients happy became a huge weight. Helpful comments and suggestions from the staff began to sting like criticism, and Paul's worth as a person became tied directly to the ups and downs of his rehab clients. When clients didn't do well, Paul didn't feel very special; when they did, Paul felt a strange vindication surrounding his life and ministry. He was a leader now, and, somehow, without realizing it, two of the 4 Deadly Ps—pleasing and performing—were now the driving force of his life and leadership.

The more Paul pursued them, the more painful life became. His relationship with his wife and children suffered. The more ministry and helping others occupied his time, the less time he had for his family. He didn't even notice, apparently. But *they* sure did. His wife and kids found it progressively harder to feed his demands for approval. Soon they could hardly relate to him. The pressure mounted.

As the ache of distance grew with his family, Paul began to remember how drugs used to lift the weight of pain . . . even if just for a while. After one exceptionally difficult day, he stopped by the store and picked up a few beers. Hiding the alcohol from his wife and family, Paul secretly drank them. Sure enough, his mood improved and the pain did diminish. The sky didn't fall, and God didn't smite him with a thunderbolt. After that, numbing became easier. He did it over and over. Eventually, he was leading the rehab program while simultaneously abusing the same drugs that his clients were. What makes his sad story even sadder is that Paul's double life had nothing to do with personal hypocrisy—he was genuinely powerless under the influence of the BEEPS that had commandeered his brain. Before it was over, he ended up back in rehab and forfeited his work and ministry. Last time I heard, the man was still adrift and angry that no one would give him back his role at the rehab center. Paul never did get it.

If you and I don't keep our motives and behaviors in check, our life and leadership will suffer. By the time our brains grab the wheel and decide to make a run for whatever BEEPS previously made the pain go away, we have already swerved waaaaay out of God's lane and into oncoming traffic. Remember, although we've been talking about someone addicted to drugs, the same dynamics are at work in codependent systems. Only close, grace-based connections with God and others can keep our motives and behaviors in check to steer us back in the right direction when we're heading the wrong way. Note to self: stay in God's lane.

GUT-GRIPPING GRACE

It goes without saying that the two guidance systems (grace and fear) cannot operate at the same time—they work in opposition to one another. Terror and anxiety, timidity and cowardice are *never* a sign of God's guidance homeward. He *never* leads His people with these devices . . . but Satan definitely does. When these emotions grip our gut and guide our decisions, you and I can be sure our enemy is leading our leadership. On the other hand, if awe, respect, and honor for God mark our grace-based leadership, you and I will recognize a steadiness of peace, joy, rest, belonging, and shalom. We will know ourselves as cherished, special, and favorite. We'll feel it in our bones, and trust me, we'll know it in our gut.

3 *Cancerous Consequences*

Think about how far you have fallen! Repent and do the works of love you did at first. I will come to you and remove your lampstand from its place of influence if you do not repent.

—REVELATION 2:5 TPT

An ounce of prevention is worth a pound of cure.

—BENJAMIN FRANKLIN

W e've all been affected by it somehow. Cancer. Upon its utterance by medical professionals, the word stuns patients around the world . . . and rightly so. As of this writing, the National Cancer Institute estimates that the United States will see 1.8 million *new* cases of the disease just this year.[9] In a myriad of forms, it cripples lives and cultures with vast physical, relational, and financial burdens. And as an illness it is unabashedly sneaky . . . shocking, really. It is a diagnosis none of us expect or welcome.

At the core, do you know what cancer is? It is an overgrowth of unhealthy cells that crowd out the normal ones wherever in the body it is present. When these rogue cells first form, cancer patients rarely know they are there. Abnormal cell growth gets a virtually undetectable head start on the body's capacity to fight it. Typically, by the time symptoms surface, the cells have multiplied exponentially and some form of major intervention is required.

While many cancers are not yet curable, cancer *is* often manageable. Caught early and well treated, people live for years—even going into remission, reversing cancer's continued growth and affording the afflicted long and happy lives. This is what every patient hopes for, but diligence is required. Diagnosis, a good medical team, and a cooperative patient who keeps to the medical protocol are essential . . . oh, and prayer . . . lots and lots of prayer.

CANCEROUS LEADERSHIP

Fear is cancerous in itself. It strikes the heart of a leader's character—deep in those long-running patterns of moral behavior. Healthy character flows from those who enjoy strong grace-based attachment and stable identities. But for those of us with nonsecure attachment and unstable identities, cancerous cells can begin to form in our motives. We fall ill. By the time we realize the cancer of fear has sickened us, we are showing symptoms that require careful diagnosis, a team of spiritual companions, and commitment to the cure.

Plenty of good leaders have gone before—leading healthy lives, consistently guided by God's grace. Think of Abraham, Abagail, Mary, and Esther, to mention a few. They were each able to "stay well." They all managed the pernicious plague of fear right—not perfectly, but healthy in the end. Their names shine in biblical history as those who submitted their lives and legacies to His glorious care. In wildly different ways, *reverential* fear moved on each one, resulting in a healthy, miraculous outcome for the people they led.

And then there are the other guys . . .

After being pestered by the Israelites for an earthly king ad nauseum, God—the heavenly King—decided to give His people what they asked for in the man Saul. Despite being the most handsome man in all of Israel and the tallest among his humble Benjamite tribe, Saul may also have been the most apprehensive pick. Yet God chose him. Why? History tells us that the man demonstrated a slow and sad progression of bad decisions at key turning points in biblical history. Below are just a few.

A LEADER IN THE LUGGAGE?

From day one, King Saul's leadership journey festered with fear. It began when his father's donkeys wandered off. Saul took his servant and went out looking for them. After searching for three days, they decided to seek out the prophet Samuel in case he could offer them some direction. Indeed, Samuel did know where the donkeys were . . . and much, much more.

Directing Saul to send his servant ahead of them, Samuel delivered the word and anointing that God had for the young man. First Samuel 10:1 (NIV) describes the story: "Then Samuel took a flask of olive oil and poured it on Saul's head and kissed him, saying, 'Has not the LORD anointed you ruler over his inheritance?'" His anointing was a picture of God's grace, expressing just how special and how favorite Saul was to Him. Samuel continued to prophesy explaining how Saul's life would be changed and empowered: "The Spirit of the LORD will come powerfully upon you, and you will prophesy with them; and you will be changed into a different person. Once these signs are fulfilled, do whatever your hand finds to do, for God is with you" (1 Samuel 10:6–7 NIV).

Wow! I mean, WOW! The people of Israel had been bugging God for years to give them a human king. Saul just learned that he was it! Again, just WOW! Do you know what happened next? After being gone for ten days, Saul headed home with the donkeys in tow. When his uncle came out to welcome him back, he asked Saul how he'd found the beasts.

Saul explained that he and his servant had sought out Samuel's help to find them . . . completely skipping the part about being chosen by God and anointed king of Israel! To make a long story short, the news eventually came out when Samuel called the tribes of Israel together to make the announcement: Saul would be their king.

As you may imagine, the crowd went wild! They thought they had just gotten what they wanted! But where *was* Saul? The people searched and searched until God stepped into their unholy hide-and-seek, revealing that Saul would be found hiding amidst the baggage. Sure enough, there he was. Not the most reassuring conduct for a national leader, right? Essentially, Saul's behavior was equivalent to an elected U.S. president deciding to skip his own inauguration and hide under the bed, hoping his new responsibilities would go away in a few days.

And for heaven's sake, why did Saul bury himself beneath the bags? Trust me when I tell you that his apprehension did not spring from a sense of false modesty. No, Saul was afraid of the duty required. Perhaps he was comfortable in his slick, fine, and beautiful life. Why would he want the weight of accountability and danger that came with the title? Hiding in the luggage may have been his way of saying, "I don't think I want this job. You've got the wrong guy." Has fear-based thinking ever made you question God's plan for your life like Saul did? Nevertheless, God—and Israel—prevailed, installing the thirty-year-old on the throne with the reassurance that he had been given everything he'd need for the task. Saul *had* the Lord's favor, but his fear blinded him to the value of the gift that had been given to him . . . and how it could carry his leadership.

BURNED BY HIS OFFERING

Soon after the beginning of his forty-two-year rule, Saul was given another opportunity to trust God's gracious direction at an essential moment. He was about to take his men into battle against the Philistines.

Before that was to happen, the prophet Samuel was supposed to come
and offer burnt offerings and fellowship offerings to God. Out-trooped,
out-charioted, and feeling a general lack of force, the king's mounting
fears seem understandable. Nonetheless, God's instructions were suc-
cinct.

Wartime tensions continued to build. The king waited. Then, Saul's
troops began to scatter. (How would you feel if you saw your men hiding in caves, thickets, and holes?) Those who *did* remain were quaking
with dread for what was to come. Where was Samuel? With the Philis-
tine enemy bearing down on them, the king lost his nerve, his patience,
and his sense of godly direction—deciding to take things into his own
hands. *Something must be done!* he must have thought to himself. First
Samuel 13:9–10 (NIV) tells what happened next: "So he said, 'Bring me
the burnt offering and the fellowship offerings.' And Saul offered up the
burnt offering. Just as he finished making the offering, Samuel arrived,
and Saul went out to greet him." Opportunity to be a faithful servant
leader—lost. When Samuel arrived, he quickly discovered that God's
instructions about the offerings had been disregarded, and Saul quickly
began making excuses:

> "When I saw that the men were scattering, and that you did
> not come at the set time, and that the Philistines were assem-
> bling at Mikmash, I thought, 'Now the Philistines will come
> down against me at Gilgal, and I have not sought the LORD's
> favor.' So I felt compelled to offer the burnt offering.

> "You have done a foolish thing," Samuel said. "You have not
> kept the command the LORD your God gave you; if you had,
> he would have established your kingdom over Israel for all
> time. But now your kingdom will not endure; the LORD has
> sought out a man after his own heart and appointed him ruler

of his people, because you have not kept the LORD's command." (1 Samuel 13:11–14 NIV)

I can relate to Saul's panic. When the pressures of life mount and it seems like people aren't coming through, sometimes it just makes more sense to do things myself. (Operating out of fear doesn't mean you are not effective in the short run.) But if my plans are not submitted to the Master Planner, graciously guided by Him, then I am being guided by fear. In this situation Saul was very effective—he won the battle, after all. As in many areas of his life, the king did just fine function out of his own resources, strengths, and giftings. (The *appearance* of success is not a good indicator of God's will for our lives and ministries.) But in this case, did he do what God asked, the *way* God asked him to do it? As leaders, we may be wildly successful— hitting our goals, touching the crowd, or reaching established attendance metrics—but we would be wise to regularly consider: *Is my vision of success aligned with God's? Are my actions humbly submitted to His authority and guidance?* Appearance is not the same as submission. If the answers to these questions don't line up, the next one should be, *What am I afraid of?*

BETTER NOT CALL SAUL

Saul's life is proof: functioning in fear doesn't permanently disqualify you or me. The Lord is exceedingly patient with us—especially when conviction or correction yields sincere repentance and a contrite heart. But that doesn't describe Saul's leadership. Just two chapters later (1 Samuel 15), in what we will call "the final episode of his anointing," God rejected Saul's kingship and self-guided warrior ways once and for all. Just before that, Samuel had yet again faithfully delivered the Lord's instructions to Saul.

As punishment for what they had done to God's people as they fled Egyptian slavery, the Amalekites were to be attacked and "utterly [destroyed]" (1 Samuel 15:3). Obediently, at least at first, Saul and his men descended on Amalek. God gave Saul and the people great victory. All was going according to plan . . . until Saul made his own. "To utterly destroy" Amalek meant to wipe them off the map without qualification. According to Scripture, Saul had no problem destroying everything "despised and worthless," but for some reason, he and his men decided to keep alive Agag (king of the Amalekites) and the best livestock (1 Samuel 15:9).

It didn't take long for the news to travel. Once again, the Lord delivered it to Samuel with yet another difficult word to share with Saul. After hearing it, Samuel spent a long and tearful night crying out to the Lord on Saul's behalf. The prophet then arose early to go and confront the king for his insubordination. When he arrived, guess where Saul had gone? According to his people, Saul had gone to Carmel and set up a monument . . . to himself! Pretending that the best animals were saved to be sacrificed to the Lord, in reality Saul made them martyrs to his own ego. God and Samuel saw right through it.

When Samuel finally caught up with Saul, at first the king played dumb, claiming he had successfully completed what the Lord had commanded him to do. But when he saw Samuel wasn't buying it, Saul started placing blame and making excuses (but with nice religious overtones, of course). Saul's fear led him to lie and try to explain his "revisions" to God's plan—it wasn't disobedience, he rationalized, it was spiritually responsible to handle things the way he did. Defensiveness and self-justification are symptoms of narcissism, not faithfulness. When the king finally *did* admit his sin, he brought the drama—hoping to redeem his reputation in front of both his prophet and his people.

> Then Saul said to Samuel, "I have sinned. I violated the Lord's command and your instructions. I was afraid of the men and so I gave in to them. Now I beg you, forgive my sin and come back with me so that I may worship the Lord."

But Samuel said to him, "I will not go back with you. You have rejected the word of the LORD, and the LORD has rejected you as king over Israel!"

As Samuel turned to leave, Saul caught hold of the hem of his robe, and it tore. Samuel said to him, "The Lord has torn the kingdom of Israel from you today and has given it to one of your neighbors—to one better than you. He who is the Glory of Israel does not lie or change his mind; for he is not a human being, that he should change his mind."

Saul replied, "I have sinned. But please honor me before the elders of my people and before Israel; come back with me, so that I may worship the Lord your God." (1 Samuel 15:24–30 NIV)

Proving that image isn't everything, Samuel called the king out for his rebellious ways in front of everyone. Yes, Israel won the Amalekite battle, but Saul lost his integrity war *and* his reign due to a personal lack of reverential fear and submission. When a leader begins to feel exposed in this way, he or she may over spiritualize things, blame the devil, deflect responsibility, or claim God directed their actions somehow—there are a lot of tactics. But this kind of behavior won't deter God. At a certain point, He *will* step in to protect His people. When that happens, you can bet that the leader's removal will be a much more public affair. That seems to have been what happened here.

Any reasonable ruler with Saul's life experience would have learned by this point what it means to have a humble and contrite heart before the Lord. (Remember: he'd been rebuked and given grace on numerous notable occasions.) Though a rational leader may not *love* the idea, sincere repentance—not to mention common sense—would demonstrate itself in support of the next ruler in line.

Apparently, Saul was a slow learner—and a not-so-reasonable predecessor. Once he discovered that David's popularity was beginning to eclipse his own, he became insane with anger. Saul couldn't stand that someone else would glean the favor that he so desperately wanted. Needless to say, he did not cooperate with God's decision to tap Jesse's youngest son for the job. Ever so *ungraciously*, the ex-anointed king moved into fear-driven hypersensitivity—raging against God's direction and against David. The deposed leader's plan? Total annihilation of his rival.

THE CRACK OF CODEPENDENCY

Sadly, leaders like King Saul are more common than you would think. While those in our day may disguise their fear-based motivations a little better, the 4 Deadly Ps are still alive and well—driving those in charge to eliminate anything or anyone who performs better, receives more approval, or throws a wrench in their plans. Performance, achievements, and approval are like religiously acceptable crack for them . . . and can keep a lot of elder boards off leaders' backs, truth be told. Whenever these drives are accommodated in life and leadership, you will find people functioning codependently.

Do you see the chaos that fear creates when this dynamic is at play? As leaders, when fear takes us away from functioning in grace, bad things happen in our lives and in the lives of those we lead. When performance, people-pleasing, pleasure-seeking, or the avoidance of pain sneak into our leadership, we end up using the people we have been called to serve. Too easily, fear crowds out our sense of God's grace—you and I forget that we are special and favorite. What appear to be innocent efforts to "do the right thing"—like offering a speedy sacrifice so the battle can go on, cherry-picking enemy livestock "for God," setting up our own altar, or (fill in the blank)—may actually be flimsy excuses for acting on our own. In reality, this kind of behavior demonstrates a gross overestimation of self and our own resources.

Can we possibly know *better* than God? Ungodly fear would like us to think so.

No matter who you are or how dynamic you may be, count on it: fear leads to tunnel vision. As it absorbs more and more of our attention, the people we lead quickly fade from view. Such blindness is just one indicator of the illness. Consciously or not, all our actions become oriented around saving our own skin—or around the fear-based motivations therein. By allowing unhealthy fears to define us, the cancer of codependency is sure to metastasize throughout the body we lead. Especially when it comes to ministry, performance and people-pleasing are a setup for the disease. It is serious, but you and I can learn to watch for symptoms so we can catch it early. We will explore these symptoms and other forms of codependency more deeply in the following chapters.

4 *The Weight of Codependency*

Ever since people first existed, they have been doing all the things we label "codependent." They have worried themselves sick about other people. They have tried to help in ways that didn't help. They have said yes when they meant no. They have tried to make other people see things their way. They have bent over backward avoiding hurting people's feelings and, in so doing, have hurt themselves. They have been afraid to trust their feelings. They have believed lies and then felt betrayed. They have wanted to get even and punish others. They have felt so angry they wanted to kill. They have struggled for their rights while other people said they didn't have any. They have worn sackcloth because they didn't believe they deserved silk.

—MELODY BEATTIE, *CODEPENDENT NO MORE*

You complete me.

—TOM CRUISE, *JERRY MCGUIRE*

U ser. When I was in high school, the term was usually delivered with a snide tone and referred to one of two kinds of people: 1) a guy or girl who slept around, using others for personal pleasure or 2) a drug addict. Neither was particularly admirable. To be called a user was definitely derogatory—you had been judged. We've already talked about it: then as now, users are heavily motivated by the weight of fear in the form of one or more of the 4 Deadly Ps. The burden is unsustainable in the context of healthy relationships. Expanded into the realm of leadership, whenever performance, people-pleasing, pleasure-seeking, or the avoidance of pain become a leader's focus, he or she crosses the line, and that leader becomes a user. No matter what they tell themselves, they become slaves to those they are called to serve. A system of codependency surfaces.

But obviously it takes two . . . or so . . .

In chapter 2 we talked about the fear-based motivations of the 4 Deadly Ps and how we readily seek to resolve them through BEEPS (Behaviors, Events, Experiences, People, or Substances). Now let's be honest: on some level, we are all users. We know how to best numb fear and pain in order to make our lives work. But as most of us have witnessed, BEEPS can hijack a person's mood, emotions, thinking, and eventually their attachments to such a degree that they create destructive, life-disrupting addiction. It's not surprising that relationships are the first casualty of any addiction. That is what we are talking about. That is the sign indicating a user has become *dependent* on his or her BEEPS of choice. All judgment has vanished. Enter the codependent.

WHAT IS CODEPENDENCY?

To help us understand the term *codependency*, in his seminal work on the topic, *Conquering Codependency*, Pat Springle explains a little history. Out of the drug-induced haze of the 1970s (about the same time I was in high school), therapists noticed a syndrome emerging.

It wasn't found in the chemically dependent, as you may expect, but in patterns of behavior surfacing within their family systems and other close relationships. These people were noted to develop "an excessive and unhealthy compulsion to rescue and take care of people"—aka codependency.[10] For them, identity was clearly dependent upon avoiding the people, emotions, and situations they feared, or upon the temporary sense of pleasure experienced by performing well and gaining the approval of others. Family members may not have touched drugs themselves, but they still shared related dysfunctional behaviors, thus winding up under the influence themselves. Researchers noticed these folks were living their lives like St. Bernard dogs in constant rescue mode—warding off or tracking down crisis after crisis in life. Codependents shared distinctive patterns of thinking, feeling, and behaving as a result of their relative's drug use.

A closer look at the word *codependency* helps explain the tangled interactions between those with addictions and others in their close relationships. When you break it down, the word *codependent* yields deep insights:

- A dependent is someone who is attached to some kind of BEEPS.
- The prefix *co* means "necessary for the functioning of . . ."

Combining these two elements, a classic understanding of the term *codependent* is revealed—a codependent individual is one who is *necessary for the functioning of* the lifestyle of a person *attached to some kind of BEEPS*. This definition makes it clear: an addict who is constantly rescued and cared for by a codependent is kept from fully experiencing the consequences of his or her behavior. Usually, without intending to, a codependent individual is actually *enabling* the person with a dependent lifestyle to continue to live that way. They are an addict's best, worst friend. Know any people like this? You can bet they are afraid of something.

Without exception, in codependent relationships and behaviors, someone must rescue or take care of another. Do you see the reward? It gives the codependent an illusion of being in control while keeping their fears away at the same time. Double bonus, for them! Underlying what seems like noble efforts to help the addict runs the recording, "I need to do this for you and I'm the only one who can," or "I know what's best for you." Well-meaning but way off, to some degree codependents allow themselves to become brainwashed by their own justifications. They behave this way out of fear. Here are three fears that are very common in such scenarios:

- *Unless I stay in control, the addict will hurt himself or herself badly.*
- *Unless I continue to do exactly what the addict wants—which is to be rescued and taken care of—he or she will leave the relationship. I will be rejected and abandoned.*
- *Unless I continue to rescue the addict and buffer the painful consequences of his or her behavior, it will cause increasing pain in the form of inability to pay bills, job loss, domestic quarrels, etc.*

In effect, a codependent's own fear-based behaviors can actually prolong an addiction in the life of another—making the problem worse for both of them. Ironically, the pursuit of the 4 Deadly Ps by both the addict *and* the codependent equally entangles them in their dysfunctional relationship. Whatever the case, let it be known: codependents are good and caring people who are trying to do the right thing. They may have grown up learning that codependent behaviors were "normal," or they may simply be trying to make sense of an addict's crazy behavior. Often, codependents are just acting out their own nonsecure attachment style or attachment pain (the distress we feel when we experience distance, separation, or loss of a previously close relationship).

Unaware that their fears and the 4 Deadly Ps are driving their behavior, codependent people can find their situation baffling. Adding to the confusion is the fact that the causes and behaviors spawned are not all the same. The myriad of types and degrees of codependent behavior, as well as environments that trigger them, are mixed. Needless to say, there is a broad spectrum of codependent behaviors to consider.

THE MYTHOLOGY OF CODEPENDENCY

In codependent relationships, the key players tell themselves a lot of different stories. We put our minds at ease with false assumptions that serve as self-justification for the dynamic. Some classic plotlines incorporate archetypal if-then thinking:

If I just love this person (check all that apply)

- well enough,
- long enough,
- strong enough,
- tough enough,

. . . then the person I'm loving will . . .

- change.
- meet my needs.
- behave well.
- love me in return.

In reality, if you or I find ourselves in a codependent relationship, what we *really feel* is fear and is more akin to the following:

If I don't love this person (again, check them if you know them)

- well enough,
- long enough,
- strong enough,
- tough enough,

... then the person I'm loving will ...
- never change or behave differently.
- never meet my needs.
- not love me in return.
- abandon me.

FAIRY-TALE THINKING: FROG KISSING, FROG KICKING

There is a lot of fear, pain, and wrong thinking rattling around in those narratives. Can you hear it? None of the outcomes have fairy-tale endings.

Most of us have heard the saying, "You have to kiss a lot of frogs before you find your prince." Codependent people tend to have a couple variations on this theme. They are either frog kissers or frog kickers. A codependent who is a frog *kisser* thinks he or she can love their dependent person enough to get them healthy and produce the necessary, spell-breaking change. The kisser is convinced that there is a beautiful prince or princess underneath the dependent's ugly exterior and once that addict is rescued, both of their lives will be great.

On the other hand, a frog *kicker* is one who becomes controlling. Realizing that they've kissed the frog enough already and no change has been produced, the kicker determines it is time for a swift kick in the froggy butt. What will the dependent frog do? Like any frog naturally would, he or she will hop. The problem is that froggy will only hop until out of boot range . . . then the movement will stop. Up until now, the frog hasn't felt the need to move, so the codependent person feels "responsible" for the frog's change. The kisser is afraid of what might happen if they don't save or help take care of the frog. Sure, the kicker cares about the little amphibian. He or she may even spiritualize their own behavior—feeling like they are doing what is best for the frog—but the bottom line is really about the frog kicker, not the frog. Though subtle, what is driving the kicker's behavior is fear.

TALE OF TWO KISSERS

Years ago, I met Donna and Chuck. They came to my office for help with their daughter Kate, a twenty-something. She had a rugged history of substance abuse, including alcohol, marijuana, and pills. What finally drove these parents to see me was her addiction to meth. Kate had minor brushes with the law. Her usual offense was breaking into the house to steal from her family members. Though the police were called a few times, her parents never wanted to press charges. As they sat across from me, they tried to explain why she was currently living in their house and described how Kate expected her parents to provide her food, even though she did not work. Donna and Chuck didn't see much of her since she stayed out late most nights (if she came home at all). Her days were spent holed up in her room—shooting meth and using alcohol or opioids to get to sleep.

Another daughter, Julia, also lived in the home. Understandably, she was sick of watching her sister use them all. Her anger smoldered as she described the incessant arguing and fighting that went on in her family home. Barely eighteen, Julia couldn't wait to get out of there, away from the chaos, and out on her own. Though her parents didn't want her to go, Julia said she was done with all the drama . . . and who could blame her?

Chuck was what I will call a passive frog kicker. Every so often, he would hit his limit with Kate and throw her out of the house . . . until he would let her come back home, that is. By his report, Chuck was fed up with Kate's behavior and would have kicked her out once and for all a long time ago, if not for Donna. Unfortunately, he and Donna couldn't see eye to eye on how to address their daughter's problem, so at this point, Chuck had resigned himself to the situation—admittedly, he had from the start of the whole, gory mess.

During one of our appointments, I tried to talk to Chuck and Donna about Kate's addiction. The room quickly chilled with tension and defensiveness. "Addiction," they said, "seems like a harsh term for what Kate has been going through." It didn't feel "appropriate" to them especially because Kate had made a confession of faith when she was younger—her character was redeemed then, after all. Listen, I get it. When we accept Christ, we take on His identity, yes, but what they were missing was that Kate's brain had been violently hijacked by behaviors and substances to which she was now attached. Because those attachments effectively displaced her love for Jesus and her family, I suggested the necessity for detox and treatment. Their response? "Well, she doesn't want to go."

I could tell you the rest of this long, sad tale of codependent denial, but the short version is Chuck and Donna didn't feel like Kate should have to do anything she didn't want to do . . . even if it was what would be best for her. As her parents, they felt she was their responsibility. With that, I challenged them: was it appropriate and responsible to let Kate shoot up in her room? Were they willing to expose themselves and Julia to the used needles lying around, as well as the many kinds of diseases associated with IV drug use? In the end, they said they would rather have Kate upstairs shooting meth than alone on the street. They decided to support her lifestyle until she was ready to make a change.

There was not much more to say. Their fears carried the weight in our conversation.

CODEPENDENCY IN SCRIPTURE

When people question where to find this in God's Word, I glibly direct them to look for anywhere fear is mentioned. Then I straighten up and get specific. We have already shown how Scripture opens with Adam and Eve making fear-based choices. Another good example is the story of Eli, *the* high priest of Israel, and his two sons. At some point in his life, it is obvious that Eli must have been dearly attached to God. He rose through the priestly ranks to a position that made him the spiritual, moral, judicial, and political leader of the Jewish people. Somehow, somewhere along the line, his loves became disordered. Once well-directed toward God, Eli's identity, judgment, and behaviors wavered.

We read in 1 Samuel 2 about his scoundrel sons, Phinehas and Hophni. Proverbially speaking, these guys were like the worst kind of preacher's kids; they were contemptuous toward the Lord and His house. Yes, they followed in their dad's footsteps to serve in the temple, but they stole the people's offerings, blasphemed God, abused worshippers, and slept with women who served at the tent of meeting. Their immoral and improper ways were no secret. (How do you think that would go over today?)

After turning a blind eye to their antics for far too long, Eli finally had enough. He called out the two boys and their wicked deeds. Not surprisingly, Phinehas and Hophni blew off Eli's rebuke and went right back to their evil ways. Apparently, the high priest responded with the equivalent of a shoulder shrug—giving up his halfhearted attempt to correct their corruption. Ah, but the God of Israel would have none of it. Soon after the failed father-and-sons conversation, a prophet arrived. He had a word for Eli. Because of his "failure to restrain them" (1 Samuel 3:13), the once great leader and his sons would reap what they had sown. The prophet continued, "'Why do you *kick* at My sacrifice and My offering which I have commanded in My dwelling place, and honor your sons more than Me, to make yourselves *fat* with the best of all the offerings of Israel My people?' Therefore the LORD God of Israel says: 'I said indeed that your house and the house of your father would walk before Me forever.' But now the LORD says: 'Far be it from Me; for those who *honor* Me I will honor, and those who despise Me shall be lightly esteemed." (1 Samuel 2:29–30, italics mine).

Three words from this passage underscore the insidious nature of codependency at work in the lives of Eli and his sons: *kick*, *fat*, and *honor*.

First on the list is *kick*. <u>*Bàat*</u> is a word used to refer to an ox that at one point has been, well, an ox—strong, healthy, and productive. That is, until it gets overindulged with food and becomes lazy. Once spoiled, the animal no longer responds to its master's commands, kicks at him, and violently attempts to shake off his yoke (Deuteronomy 32:15). The word was, Eli and his sons had become like the disobedient, self-indulgent ox. Eli, Phinehas, and Hophni pursued their own gain—taking for granted their leadership and God-given position as special and favorite. Stepping away from a once holy and vibrant relationship with the Lord, the three chose instead to use their station for their own evil purposes.

Next, let's look at the term *fat*. This word is translated from the Hebrew word *bârâ'*, meaning "to create." Starting in Genesis 1:1, the word is used to describe God's creative activity. We can also find it used to describe clearing timber to plant crops or make a new place to live. Interestingly, this reference is the only point in the Old Testament where this word, bârâ', translates negatively to mean "fat" (overweight). The excessive, unhealthy, and indulgent lifestyle of Eli and his sons exceeded the sacred leadership boundaries God had put in place to protect His people. Instead, these priests willfully created an artificial space to do what they wanted in the temple—using their religious position as a means of justifying and covering up their rebellious behavior. Quite literally, they behaved as if they were above the Law, exempt from correction. But God was not to be mocked. Ruin soon followed for the three . . . and Eli enabled it all.

Finally, there is the definition of *honor*. The Hebrew word, *kâbad*, means "to be heavy, numerous, or weighty." Quite literally, Eli misplaced the weight of his attachment with God. Instead, he gave too much weight to his fears about correcting his sons and not enough weight about what God asked him to do. As a result, his boys' feelings tipped the scales. Evidently, how Phinehas and Hophni reacted to correction or rejected him meant more to Eli than the place God held in his heart.

His fears about his sons seemed to matter more than doing things God's way. When you consider the high priest's life up to this point and all that God had done to demonstrate His favor with him, it is hard to understand why Eli chose to let his rogue sons influence him so heavily. It was a massive misplacement of his relational priorities. BEEPS took the trio down—distorting, dictating, and manifesting in profoundly destructive behaviors. The great religious leader was misled—away from attachment with God. If the 4 Deadly Ps and BEEPS can mislead a high priest, you and I had best beware: it matters what we give weight to in our lives.

THE WEIGHT OF PERSONAL EXPECTATIONS

Most of us hold some form of personal expectations—the way we *think* things should be. If we are not mindful of the motivations behind them, our expectations, before we know it, can anchor themselves in codependency and drop us to bottom-dwelling behaviors. When we get out of balance with God—more motivated by our own fears than love for Him—that is when our expectations will run amuck. A while back, this happened to me.

I had a job opportunity at a highly regarded rehab center. They did an amazing job of saving and restoring people who were on the brink of self-destruction. I had worked and trained with some of their staff in the past. Going in, I was sure I could contribute and was eager to learn from the tremendous treatment program they had built.

Fairly quickly, I noted the strong scent of a high-performance attitude in the air. On the surface, a demand for loyalty and excellence within the approval-based culture was clear. But the longer I was there, the more I recognized that shame and anger were undergirding the center's hard-driving culture. Unspoken expectations put upon staff by higher-ups sent the message that if we didn't do the "right thing" in any given situation, we would be deemed incompetent and rebuked. It didn't matter to them if we hadn't been taught or trained regarding what those things were. Somehow we were expected to know. Pleasing, performing, and pain avoidance kept the staff on edge most of the time. Daily we would each hope the boss was in a good mood and that our supervisors were pleased with our work.

As time went by, I got sucked in and began asking myself telltale codependent questions:

- How can I look like I know what I'm doing?
- Can I trust the guys I work with to be authentic?
- What is the best way to stay out of trouble in this situation?

At the time, these seemed like good questions to ask. I wanted to succeed—to support the leadership team, grow my professional expertise, and serve the rehab patients well. But the longer I was there, the clearer it became: my growing fear-driven, punishment-avoidant orientation reflected a sick environment. As I internalized the stress of the workplace, I began to feel physically sick too. I developed an unusual allergy to wheat, lost thirty pounds, and experienced intestinal problems.

Eventually (just about the same time as I began learning some of the deep things I've shared here about grace and grace-based attachment), a position opened up within a different area of the rehab center. Outside of work, as grace unfolded to me, I began to recognize the important role that attachment plays in our spiritual transformation.

What seemed like impossibly high standards of the rehab center had caused me to question my personal worth. You see, up to that point I had been letting my need for approval and significance define me. My own fear of failure to perform up to my employer's expectations created immense self-doubt.

Slowly it dawned on me: through His grace, Jesus had already provided for my need for approval and significance. I didn't need anything from my boss. When I finally realized that my micromanipulations did not get me any further than the place I already held in His heart, my need for approval and significance from my job no longer defined me. I could fully love and serve the people I worked with as an outpouring of who God made me to be. Did you catch the shift? My motivation moved from fear-based to grace-based, and my methods of ministry to those in recovery shifted too. I was able to stay another couple of years before God moved me on.

Those days changed me forever. I am grateful for my time there, and I still believe in the work of that treatment center. Results demonstrated in the lives of their patients speak for themselves: the center does life-changing restorative work helping people. Most of all, I am thankful that God used my experience there to help clarify my own struggles with the 4 Deadly Ps. What I took away was foundational in my life with God going forward. The bridge from heavy, fear-based to His love is one every codependent person must cross . . . including me. Otherwise, we run the risk of getting sidetracked from our calling.

A WEIGHTED VEST FOR YOUR SOUL

Have you ever tried to work out with a weighted vest on? (A weighted vest is a sadistic device worn to add extra body weight in order to make a workout harder.) Codependency is like a weighted vest for your soul. Putting it on creates resistance to a grace-based reality of life with God. As you and I press through reps of unhealthy relational cycles and gut out hard things in codependent ways, we may as well strap another hundred pounds to our belts. That is what it is like when we behave as if it is on us to save or care for another.

God doesn't ask us to bear the load of our own fears alone, nor the feelings and reactions of others. In fact, He would prefer that you and I remain so connected to him that *He* determines what to pick up and carry *for* us. None of this is ours to lug about, and yet somehow many of us have gotten the very incorrect idea that helping dependent people is the "right"—or worse, the "Christian"—thing to do. Fittingly, the compassionate part of Jesus that lives in each of us wants to help others in ways that are life-giving. However, rushing blindly into those situations to rescue and care for people without checking our 4 Deadly Ps will perpetuate the problem. It is essential that we slow down to consider our motivation for helping. Otherwise, you and I may mistake mercy for a fear-based reaction—when we react, we put on the weight vest.

I can already hear you wondering, *So how do we love, care for, and serve others without becoming codependent?* Don't worry. We will get there, but first it is essential to consider whether you or I may be wearing unnecessary weight. Does the person who frequently weighs heavy on your heart really need the Savior, or have you decided to shoulder the responsibility yourself?

In life and in leadership roles, no one but Jesus gets the role of Savior. When you or I let our own fear-based motivations drive us to become a savior to others, we find ourselves flailing about, clumsily kicking at God's grace. And after a while it will feel like we are doing it wearing leg weights. Eventually, all our well-intended efforts wear us out—physically, emotionally, and spiritually. (Remember Eli's word about the stubborn ox?) This is what happens when codependency gets confused with mercy. You and I are bound to hurt ourselves and anyone else involved. If we are honest, I think we can admit that it has happened to a lot of us. From a biblical perspective and for the good of others, it is important to understand what mercy is in God's sight and how He applies it. Then we will be readily able to recognize the times it is called for, as well as the times when it is inappropriate. That way, you and I can be sure to keep the weight right where it belongs: on Him.

5   *Oh, Mercy! The Confusion of Codependency*

"O Gandalf, best of friends, what am I to do? For now I am really afraid. What am I to do? What a pity that Bilbo did not stab that vile creature, when he had a chance!"
"Pity? It was Pity that stayed his hand. Pity, and Mercy: not to strike without need. And he has been well rewarded, Frodo. Be sure that he took so little hurt from the evil, and escaped in the end, because he began his ownership of the Ring so. With Pity."

—J.R.R. TOLKIEN, *THE FELLOWSHIP OF THE RING*

Let the wicked forsake his way,
And the unrighteous man his thoughts;
Let him return to the LORD,
And He will have mercy on him;
And to our God,
For He will abundantly pardon.

—ISAIAH 55:7

No matter what part of the country you are from, homelessness is harsh. In the tough and intemperate climate of Washington D.C., it is an especially bleak existence. The city is home to one of the country's largest homeless populations, each person with a story all their own. I lived in a suburb of D.C. for twenty-six years. Part of that time, I worked with a ministry that served the homeless, seeing their faces and understanding their circumstances. Among my kind and brilliant coworkers, there was a shared motivation: "This should not be." So, out of seemingly tireless and sincere compassion, we offered the people who came needing help a warm welcome, a handsome place to stay, connection with medical care, and other necessary services. The compassion extended was beautiful. Over time the program shifted to work primarily with people suffering addictions.

We had a strict policy: no substances in the house and no coming in drunk or drugged. Regardless of this boundary, something was missing. No part of our assistance addressed the primary problem behind what brought each of these people to our door—what was behind their eyes and lodged in their hearts. As their overriding compulsions to drink, drug, or drift into mental illness resurfaced, these people would return to the streets.

Our program was not the only one approaching the crisis this way. Other people running shelters and health care programs would report that they, too, did not allow substance abuse on their property. Yet they resisted requiring residents to attend programs like AA or rehab. Some even elevated their idea of mercy to include looking the other way when people ignored the rules. All of it sent the wrong message to those residents working hard to stay sober. In essence, this approach reduced our ministries to warehouses—we sheltered and enabled people in the misused name of mercy.

Oh, mercy! How does this go on? Well, it all boils down to a gross misunderstanding. Codependents are constantly trying to make sense of the senseless. You see, they fancy themselves to be problem solvers. In their own minds they've worked out complicated equations to avoid their fears—solving for *y*. Perhaps it is more accurate to say codependents work their lives around *why* and *how* things should be handled in order to set a dependent person's life aright—and consequently also their own. Consciously or not, their calculations eliminate the need for God—His mercy *and* His grace. I mean, who needs either if you and I are really the ones who "know what is best," right?

To be clear: codependency is a spectrum. Each of us has a place on it. We are built to reflect God's loving-kindness, but you can be sure that if you find yourself bone-tired, bitter, and resentful, you are carrying some of the weight of a codependent disposition. Our fears set up the whole dynamic. That being the case, how can we

- tell when we—or someone close to us—is acting in this fashion?
- steer clear of the destructive tendency to rescue?
- determine when God is calling us to help someone?

These answers and more can be uncovered by a simple biblical study of mercy.

DIGGING UP MERCY

Call me "different," but I enjoy learning the etymology of words—their origin and evolution. Word studies in Scripture are of particular interest to me. It feels like an archeological adventure. Think *Raiders of the Lost Ark*, only with words. After just a little digging, we can unearth God's intent from a word's semantic range and context. Quite literally, there is a body of information just waiting to be discovered about mercy. Though not buried too deeply, I venture to guess that most of us have never excavated these ideas before.

Old Testament Mercy

In the Old Testament, primarily three words are used for mercy. What jumps out to me here is how each describes a physical posture.

The first, *chêsêd*, is the Hebrew word for loving-kindness that denotes favor, a good and merciful deed done for another. One of its primitive roots, *châsad*, is a kind and merciful gesture shared between friends—**bowing the neck** as an expression of humility. When I feel this kind of mercy toward you, I want to bless you. Both of us are in a posture of humility.

The second word used, *chânan*, describes a loving-kindness that **stoops to bow to someone from a lower position.** This kind of mercy requires the yielding of a superior person in order to bestow it upon one in need. Again, it encompasses an element of humility, favor, and pity that is freely given. If I show you this kind of mercy, I do so with a heart that desires to lift you up.

The third Old Testament word for mercy is *râcham*. *Râcham* reveals a picture of loving compassion that **holds another dearly.** When I am open to receive your close, warm, and yielding gesture of mercy, I am able to receive the deep sympathy and sorrow you are offering to ease your affliction or relieve your suffering. In Scripture, this word is most commonly used when the Lord showed compassion upon someone who had done nothing to merit such comfort.

Each of these Old Testament terms contains a physical picture of what God sees when a person is ready to receive mercy. By these definitions, the person needing mercy is willing to bow or be held. When a person does not bow, Scripture calls them "stiff-necked." According to the standard of God's Word, showing mercy to such a person is misguided. A person who is bowing *is* in a position ready to receive mercy. Don't forget those word pictures as we move on.

New Testament Mercy

Now, let's excavate for what New Testament writings reveal about mercy.

Throughout its pages, the most broadly used word for mercy in the New Testament is the Greek word *eleos*. Compassion and tenderness mark its use. Grace and mercy are similar and related—it's hard to find one without the other in Scripture. While grace relates to being God's favorite, mercy describes the kind of heartrending compassion God has for us despite our sin and its consequences in our lives. Rightly given, His mercy is offered *to alleviate our suffering*. Because we live in a sinful world, mercy is our ongoing need, and humility is the only posture that can truly receive it.

Scripturally, *splagchnizomai* is a closely related Greek word that denotes a visceral, gut-wrenching reaction to the suffering or circumstance of another person or group. Driven by pity or sympathy, such an inner move to compassion makes your insides flip.

Eureka! Our quest for answers about this is over! From our studious search, we can announce the treasure that we have unearthed: healthy (non-codependent) New Testament expressions of mercy! As described in the Old Testament, the act of bowing before someone—no matter what their status—assumes an attitude and posture of great humility. Furthermore, receiving hugs full of compassion requires a genuinely sober yielding indicative of a willingness to receive. Without this posture, no one can receive the poignant compassion God and others feel for them. Take my word for it, attempting to pour out mercy on a stiff-necked, prideful person will backfire—such a person will be unable to receive it. On the other hand, one who is desirous of mercy (and truly ready for it) will show no hesitation to surrender their will, bow down, and be held by one who offers godly mercy.

To recap: if you and I want to be sure when and how to rightly extend God's mercy to another, here is a simple, balanced equation:

Old Testament Posture + New Testament Compassionate Response
= Healthy Opportunity for Divine Mercy

BROKE OR BROKEN?

Think about the story of the prodigal son. He left for the bright lights of big-city living all proud, entitled, and sure of himself. Middle Eastern culture considers what he did—asking for his inheritance early—to be the equivalent of saying, "I wish you were dead, Dad." Chutzpah is what that is! In village culture, spending that inheritance outside his village and culture was considered the ultimate act of disrespect to the *whole* tribe. This behavior added insult to injury. And according to the custom of the day, the prodigal could have been killed before his sandals hit the road out of town. For whatever reason, his father gave him his portion and waved good-bye.

Eventually, when the boy's money ran out and his taste for pig slop waned, there came a moment of clarity: *I hate my life! What am I doing?* Flat broke, he determined to secure a better life for himself as a servant in his father's household. So, the wayward boy turned back toward home—not to apologize but to ask for a job. Imagine his posture as he came down the road. Embarrassed, dejected, weary, eyes turned to the ground. Maybe he was humiliated . . . but he was probably not yet humbled. Through the sting of hot tears, do you suppose he looked up long enough to see his father running toward him?

His dad must have been looking for the boy because Scripture says that from a long way off he saw the once-wandering lad heading back home. Aside from the presumed joy of his son's return, there is good reason to suspect that the father ran to greet him in order to get there before the villagers tore him apart with a vengeance. Once he reached his boy, it was no cold greeting either—the father gave him a full and robust embrace. Do you suppose it was *then* that the prodigal went from just broke to humbly broken? Whatever the case, he was welcomed home. Essentially the father told him, "You were lost! Now you're back! I want to celebrate your return and restore you to your place! Look, everyone, my child is alive and well!" (Luke 15:24)

Stop for a second. You and I need to feel that like the prodigal did.

A lot is said about his turnaround and the older brother's ungracious welcome, but have you ever thought about this dad's *healthy* demonstration of mercy? This whole story was a textbook opportunity for codependency? Instead, as hard and scary as it must have been to watch his son head off in the wrong direction, the father let him go with grace. The boy "had his own story to write," as they say—consequences and all. Wisely, the man understood: this prodigal must comprehend his father's grace in order to grasp the judicious roof of mercy under which he had been living. Only then could he freely choose to return to its foundation of compassionate love. No fear or control exerted by the father would resolve the issues vying for his son's heart. The son must do his work—in the poverty of homelessness, ugly drunkenness, and stinking pig slop, if necessary. But rest assured, the father deeply grieved the empty place at the table where his son belonged.

GOD *IS* THIS KIND OF MERCY

At least a few times throughout our lives, each of us wanders off on our own, prodigal-like. As part of who He is, God patiently longs to welcome us home—to offer His extravagant protection and mercy toward you and me. Because it is who He *is*, God can't help Himself! Full to overflowing—our Father longs to run to us and show us compassion in all of its forms. Exodus 33:19 describes His delight: "Then He said, 'I will make all My goodness pass before you, and I will proclaim the name of the LORD before you. I will be gracious to whom I will be gracious, and I will have compassion [mercy] on whom I will have compassion [mercy].'" It is His character.

Rather than deal with us out of anger or exasperation, He deals with us as a kind and tender and loving father—giving grace and mercy liberally and for our good growth. Does that describe your image of Him? If not, let me encourage you to reenvision God and yourself through the eyes of grace.

CANDIDATES FOR MERCY

Sometimes God goes out of His way to publicly show mercy. The way we decide to live will position us for it. When you or I make mistakes, isn't this good to know? The Lord seems especially inclined to extend His mercy to two types of people:

1. Those who honor, give weight to, and reverentially fear Him. The Bible says He shows it "to thousands, to those who love [Him] and keep [His] commandments" (Exodus 20:6).

2. Those who turn to Him in repentance, confess, and forsake their sin. As Isaiah 55:7 reads, "Let the wicked forsake his way, and the unrighteous man his thoughts; Let him return to the LORD, and He will have mercy on him; and to our God, for He will abundantly pardon."

MERCY AND TRUTH

Especially when we are talking about codependency, it is essential to remember that expressions of godly mercy cannot happen apart from truth. But for those with the spiritual *gift* of mercy, the line may easily blur. With this, I can see your head tilt in confusion: *Isn't the Christian answer always bringing help and comfort to others?* I hear your bewilderment, and trust me, it is common. Remember what we learned about those positioned to receive mercy? The connection between mercy and truth is undeniable, so if I sincerely desire mercy, my posture, attitudes, and actions will match my words. Proverbs 16:6 gets straight to the point: "In mercy and truth atonement is provided for iniquity; and by the fear of the LORD one departs from evil." My Southern friends would say, "You can't walk North and talk South."

Want an example? If I habitually yell at my wife (or _____; fill in the blank with your own sin pattern), then express my regret and apologize, God will graciously work to teach me the right way to handle my temper (or_____; fill in the blank with your own issue). However, if I forsake His guidance, returning to the habit as part of a cycle, things are bound to get harder. You see, going back to my yelling over and over demonstrates that I am "stiff-necked"—a poser forsaking God's generous compassion. I don't genuinely seek change, and in effect, my actions are nothing more than a manipulative con. In recovery speak, we call that "being broke but not broken." Returning to the wisdom of Proverbs, chapter 28, verse 13 is direct about it: "He who covers his sins will not prosper, but whoever confesses and forsakes them will have mercy."

When you or I know something is wrong in what we are doing, and yet we keep doing it, our hearts become hardened to our sin. We are not broken for what breaks God's heart. But when we allow the truth of God to X-ray our lives and set what is broken, we will become aligned with His mercy. He has no illusions about us. Throughout His Word, God welcomes our mercy-seeking, sinful selves back to His throne of grace. "Have mercy on me!" (Psalm 6:2), "Have mercy on us!" (Psalm 123:3), "Have mercy!" the psalmist begs. Understanding what is at stake here, we ask God to bow His merciful head in the direction of our repentant hearts. But will He? We find our assurance in Hebrews 4:16: "Let us therefore come boldly to the throne of grace, that we may obtain mercy and find grace to help in time of need."

MERCY, YOU, AND ME

Since He *is* mercy, God expects this trait to be reflected in our character as well: "He has shown you, O man, what is good; and what does the LORD require of you but to do justly, to love mercy, and to walk humbly with your God?" (Micah 6:8). As God directs, you and I need to feel the tenderness of mercy for our sin, and hold the same compassion for one another.

Jesus showed up on the scene to serve adrift sinners, not the line-walking, religiously self-righteous. Knowing us better than you or I would like to admit, He spelled it out in Matthew 9:13: "But go and learn what this means: 'I desire mercy and not sacrifice.' For I did not come to call the righteous, but sinners, to repentance." From what I've seen, we could use a refresher in this lesson, not just once but again and again.

THE HARD PART: BAD CANDIDATES

With a seemingly well-defined understanding of God's kind and generous mercy in hand, now comes the hard part: some people are bad candidates to receive it. Again, acting as a loving father, there are times when our heavenly Father says, "No more!" For the good of everyone involved, there are limits. When people persist in doing evil—enjoying and abusing mercy with no change—or refuse to show mercy to another, there comes a time when the spigot of His mercy will crank closed. Not a drop will drip in their direction. When chronic evil or merciless behavior occurs, habitually separating them from the truth, one of two things may happen:

- Those pursuing the fear-based 4 Deadly Ps (aka "users," as described in the previous chapter) will continue to their destruction.
- Codependents will continue to comply with their fear-based justifications and to aid the user.

Unfortunately, sometimes both occur.

I'm sure such was the case for the Jews in Isaiah 9. Taking advantage of God's mercy, they persisted in ignoring His direction. Though God tried many times to correct His chosen ones, their pride and arrogance continued. Stiff-necked and unrelenting, God's people wanted to fix and rebuild things the way *they* liked them and keep going. The Lord addressed their arrogance by sending hard times on them (Isaiah 9:8–10): "The Lord sent a word against Jacob, and it has fallen on Israel. All the people will know—Ephraim and the inhabitant of Samaria—who say in pride and arrogance of heart: 'The bricks have fallen down, but we will rebuild with hewn stones; the sycamores are cut down, but we will replace them with cedars.'"

Still, the people didn't pay attention, so God sent other countries against them. It may come as no surprise, but in verses 11–13 of Isaiah 9 we continue to read about their unrelenting disobedience: "Therefore the Lord shall set up the adversaries of Rezin against him, and spur his enemies on, the Syrians before and the Philistines behind; and they shall devour Israel with an open mouth. For all this His anger is not turned away, but His hand is stretched out still. For the people do not turn to Him who strikes them, nor do they seek the Lord of hosts."

Finally, as a result of their own unstoppable, wicked pursuits, Isaiah 9:14–17 describes how God cut them off: "Therefore the Lord will cut off head and tail from Israel, palm branch and bulrush in one day. The elder and honorable, he is the head; the prophet who teaches lies, he is the tail. For the leaders of this people cause them to err, and those who are led by them are destroyed. Therefore, the Lord will have no joy in their young men, nor have mercy on their fatherless and widows; for everyone is a hypocrite and an evildoer, and every mouth speaks folly. For all this His anger is not turned away, but His hand is stretched out still."

Because of their utter disregard for God and His mercy, divine judgment fell against an entirely corrupt culture. Make no mistake: there are times when a person or a culture can mask their corruption to the point of their own demise. Regardless of slick appearances and righteous self-justifications, God is not mocked. Now comes the part where I'm going to ask you to wake up and consider this as a leader: is any part of this behavior reflected in the culture of your church, leadership team, or community? God cares when His mercy is twisted or disregarded.

In case you think this was an unusual occurrence, something similar happened in Jeremiah 13:9–14. Yet again, despite God's love and promises for their good, His people refused to listen: "'For as the sash clings to the waist of a man, so I have caused the whole house of Israel and the whole house of Judah to cling to Me,' says the LORD, 'that they may become My people, for renown, for praise, and for glory; but they would not hear'" (Jeremiah 13:11). Though our ruin is not His heart for us, God knows how we are made. For ourselves and those we lead, you and I are wise to abandon our excuses, heed His correction, and humbly esteem His mercy. Left to our own devices, we will learn things do not end well. Jeremiah 13:14 closes this episode with a dire warning for any who disregard His attempts to bestow mercy: "'And I will dash them one against another, even the fathers and the sons together,' says the LORD. 'I will not pity nor spare nor have mercy, but will destroy them.'"

If you've ever received mercy, appreciate it—don't take it for granted. When God says he wants things out of our lives and proximity, you and I need to listen well. No hedging. No self-justification. Simply obey. Things become idols when we don't. Though His heart is that we will turn from these things, God will eventually leave us to our own devices. He is consistent with His Word: "Those who regard worthless idols forsake their own mercy" (Jonah 2:8). Just as a "user" needs a committed community for a breakthrough, the hard-hearted, unmerciful believer requires one as well. By humbly remembering and sharing about the mercy we have been shown, we will forsake any bent toward religious judgmentalism and draw others to the goodness of God's heart.

SOWING AND REAPING

Does that get your attention? It sure got mine. This is serious business. Grace calls us the Lord's favorite. Mercy reflects His desire to demonstrate this truth in our lives. If you and I remain unbowing and unsurrendered to *His* will, we will reap what we sow.

His heart for us never changes. It is we who have lost track of our First Love. Someone once said, "Sometimes God's mercy is His judgment." Think of it this way: You are a kid playing in the middle of the street. Like most children, your parents have set rules about playing outside, crossing in crosswalks, staying in the driveway to play, etc. Still, you choose to disregard them. It isn't the first time. Suddenly, your dad runs out in the front yard, wildly waving his arms—urgently yelling at you to get out of the street. A trash truck is barreling toward you. When he reaches you in the middle of the road, he scoops you up in his arms and bounds toward the curb like a superhero. Is this punishment or care? You can listen, or you can keep doing what you want, but don't be fooled. Your Father knows best. You and I are dearly beloved with a free will. Ongoing disobedience reaps consequences—and that grieves the heart of God.

MISAPPLIED MERCY

When snagged by personal idols and addictions, God knows that withdrawing His mercy is necessary for some to return to Him. Galatians 6:7–10 (NIV) explains, "Do not be deceived: God cannot be mocked. A man reaps what he sows. Whoever sows to please their flesh, from the flesh will reap destruction; whoever sows to please the Spirit, from the Spirit will reap eternal life. Let us not become weary in doing good, for at the proper time we will reap a harvest if we do not give up. Therefore, as we have opportunity, let us do good to all people, especially to those who belong to the family of believers."

That last bit—"let us do good to all people"—is where many misapply mercy. When people we love make bad choices, what does that mean for us? It may mean we must *not* help. For example,

- *not* calling the boss to make another excuse for why your hungover spouse missed work
- *not* giving rent money to your brother who never seems to have enough money but refuses to stick to a budget
- *not* providing shelter and food to a child who is purposely unemployed (or their lack of motivation keeps them underemployed) yet old enough to be on their own
- *not* continuing to work harder to solve problems for someone who is not adequately doing the same for themself
- *not* keeping quiet when someone you love is continuing sinful habits that are harmful to themselves or the greater good
- *not* tolerating verbal, emotional, physical, or spiritual abuse in the relationship, whether in marriage or otherwise

To do otherwise is to act in fear and misapply God's mercy. Though the outcome is not up to you and me, sometimes we must get out of the way and allow the dynamic of sowing and reaping to occur. God is the perfect dad who knows the difference between when we are cooperatively learning from our mistakes and when our stubbornness requires Him to say, "No way, Jose!" It is incumbent upon each of us to prayerfully discern what this means in our lives and relationships.

When we casually dole out mercy or mishandle it by acting in fear, you and I behave codependently. The consequences are significant to us—*and* to the one we want to "help." In the long run, it accomplishes the *opposite* of what we want. In reality, our behavior has some predictable outcomes. It will

- interrupt the law of sowing and reaping in another's life
- intercept the consequences of their negative behavior—making it harder for God to get their attention
- insulate the other person from the pain that could lead to their positive growth and change
- set us up, as the codependent, to reap the mental, emotional, spiritual, relational, social, vocational, and family costs of the other person's actions

A CODEPENDENT PORTRAIT OF MISPLACED MERCY

All codependents really want is to create a safe place in the middle of their fears. Lauren would tell you herself, that is her story. Her husband, Kyle, was a drug addict. Together they had three small children. When the fury of her fears drove her into counseling, I got to know her . . . but it took her a while to get there. For years, she had been naïve to the ways of addiction. Though she knew Kyle had a substance problem, Lauren thought that with the support of extended family they could beat it. Money always seemed to be tight, groceries were a stretch, but Lauren was determined. After all, she was raised to believe that families must stick together at all costs.

As things unfolded, she found out that Kyle's family had been a massively codependent force in his addiction almost from the beginning. Seemingly at all costs, they wanted to keep things looking "normal." "No one needs to know that anything is wrong," they would say. "We'll help to take care of things. Despite years marked by numerous trips to rehab, check fraud, job bouncing, and jail, Lauren went along with their attempts to problem-solve and get him out of trouble. The mornings he couldn't get up for work, she would make excuses with Kyle's latest boss to help keep him employed and keep food on the table for the family. Sure, he sowed bad seed, but the misguided efforts of those close to him—including his wife—offset the consequences of his destructive behavior. Why quit?

All this time, Lauren had just been trying to be a good mom—to keep her family together and her kids safe. *Everybody knows Jesus hates divorce, and kids need their dad, right?* The opposite of fixing things, her way of thinking sustained Kyle's addictive behavior—imprisoning Lauren and her children in a chronically sick system. Kyle had no incentive to work on *his* stuff. All he had to do was manipulate her, and he could get what he wanted: the drugs. He used the best part of Lauren's heart against her.

At last it became obvious: her trauma was bound to continue if *she* didn't get healthy. Almost to the very end, Lauren believed that God would swoop in with a miracle and restore them all. Sadly, it never happened.

Their marriage devolved to an intolerable level: a domestic violence episode forced the extent of Lauren's codependence into the light. Counseling provided her a newfound understanding of the problem and the help of a good mentor. Lauren gradually realized that as long as she depended on Kyle to do what she wanted him to do, *she* was allowing herself to be a big part of the problem. When she finally determined to face her fears of the future and the pain of abandonment that loomed, the chains of codependency began to break apart. It wasn't easy, but her healing came. Codependency almost killed her, but after what seemed like an eternity of married life, Lauren plainly saw how she had been misapplying mercy.

Wrongly given mercy reaps its own infested harvest. It is easy to see how this is true in personal relationships. Still, you and I must be equally aware of how it can show up in ministry, professional, and helping relationships. It can quickly lead to burnout or what is known as "compassion fatigue." Here are some warning signs of codependency to watch for:

- Feeling increasingly hopeless, helpless, and victimized
- Becoming more controlling as you work even harder to stop, manage, or minimize the damage
- Developing increased levels of health-related problems
- Desperately grasping at straws—including "spiritual" interventions—in order to make the pain stop
- Becoming so stressed that it is tough to manage life, work, and family
- Turning relationally desperate/toxic without ever intending to do so
- Feeling so ashamed that you isolate yourself from others
- Spending most of your mental energy focusing on another person's behavior
- Noticing an increase in your levels of anger and/or depression

If any of these looks familiar, go back and check yourself. Which of the 4 Deadly Ps (Pleasing, Performing, Pain Avoidance, Pleasure Seeking) are you operating out of concerning this relationship or group? What fears are activated in you? How are these manifesting in your relationship with this individual or community? What weight are you carrying that doesn't belong to you? You must step back, assess the situation, and take a deep breath.

No question, mercy has become a convoluted topic in the minds of some people, but it's actually quite simple: if you're functioning in grace, ask God about *every* opportunity to show mercy *before* you blindly offer it. He sees the posture of the heart—yours, mine, *and* the needy candidate. Let's quit hurting people with our knee-jerk inclinations to help indiscriminately.

In the end, true mercy requires the courage to face our fears. There is nothing milquetoast about it. Far from timid, unassertive, or spineless, it takes grit—grit to discern when it's called for and guts to hold the line when it's not. To rescue another from their brokenness ahead of God's timing is to inflict greater injury. And, we truly don't want to do that!

6 *Warnings from a Man on the Beach*

I was angry with my friend;
I told my wrath, my wrath did end.
I was angry with my foe:
I told it not, my wrath did grow.

And I waterd it in fears,
Night and morning with my tears:
And I sunned it with smiles,
And with soft deceitful wiles.

And it grew both day and night.
Till it bore an apple bright.
And my foe beheld it shine,
And he knew that it was mine.

And into my garden stole,
When the night had veild the pole;
In the morning glad I see;
My foe outstretched beneath the tree.

—WILLIAM BLAKE, "A POISON TREE"

*Then the disciples came to him and asked, "Do you know that
the Pharisees were offended when they heard this?"
He replied, "Every plant that my heavenly Father has not planted will be pulled up by the roots. Leave them; they are blind
guides. If the blind lead the blind, both will fall into a pit."
Peter said, "Explain the parable to us."*

—MATTHEW 15:12–15 NIV

I magine yourself on a beautiful Caribbean shore. The water is crystal
blue, transparent enough to see shells and sea life living beneath the
waves. The musky sweetness of tropical flowers wafts through the
air, which just happens to be the perfect beach-going temperature. Bare-
footed, you pad your way along the soft, sandy shoreline for a while, letting the waves skim your toes. You walk the undisturbed stretch of beach
for quite a distance, enjoying the view until you tire out. Ahead, you spy
a large tree up near the water's edge with broad leaves and beautiful fruit
weighting its boughs. It seems like you've landed on Eden's shore! Deciding to linger beneath the shade of its branches for a bit, you wander up,
take a seat near the trunk, and begin to recline against it.

Suddenly, out of nowhere, a man comes running at you. Absolutely
frantic, he is waving his arms to alert you. *"STOP! NO! DON'T! WATCH
OUT! IT'S DEADLY!"* Catching yourself as you start to lean back to position yourself against the trunk, you jolt to your feet, anxious and afraid.
What in the world is going on?! Heart racing, your eyes dart around, trying
to find the danger. You don't see anything that could kill you.

The man continues with alarm, "Look up! This is a manchineel
tree!"

"A . . . whaaaa . . . ?" you stammer. Still on high alert, you look up
and blink inquisitively.

"Let's move out from under it," he says, urgently ushering you back into the sun. "Some people call it 'arbol de la muerte,' the 'tree of death.' It is one of the deadliest fruit trees on the planet. You didn't eat anything, did you? The poison killed Ponce de Leon. Please tell me you didn't touch it?!"

"No," you reassure him. "I was just about to lean back for a little rest, that's all."

"Gracias, a Dios! It would have killed you. The fruit is sweet to the taste, but it will strangle you. The smoke from its wood is blinding, and its sap is so toxic that it burns and melts skin like acid. Even sheltering under one of those during a storm can poison you when the leaves drip with rain. Whatever you do while you're here, watch out for these! This should have been marked. You could have been killed!"

Okay now. Come back to me, reader.

Manchineel trees are for real. You can find them mixed in with mangroves in Florida and throughout the Caribbean. For obvious reasons, they are difficult to remove. Because they help prevent beach erosion, they are usually marked and left alone. They serve a purpose, but I'm not sure I think it is a reasonable trade-off for the danger they pose. Attractive but deadly, there is nothing subtle about this life-threatening natural hazard. From root to treetop, every aspect of a manchineel tree is toxic. You don't dare mess with one.

When leadership grows from the roots of fear and codependency, it is much the same.

Think of me as the man running toward you on the beach.

Your life and leadership depend on whether you heed the warning I'm about to give you: unaddressed, fear and codependency will burn or kill you, the people you lead, and your entire organization. The danger is grossly underestimated. As we saw in chapter 4, kissing or kicking others to gain compliance never works for a leader—at least not for long.

WHAT LEADERSHIP SMELLS LIKE

Remember the 4 Deadly Ps? Motivated by people-pleasing or performance, a leader who is attached to BEEPS (Behaviors, Events, Experiences, People, or Substances) will exploit people—setting up a manipulative, codependent culture, intentionally or not. They can look so good on the outside too. Basing their identity on highs born from image, success metrics, control, religious rationale, and problem mitigation, such a leader treats both those they lead and those they serve as nothing more than pawns in the game. If these characteristics turn up in the life of your leadership, call a spiritual hazmat team, quick!

When the rancid smell of codependency tinges the air of leadership, too many of us have learned to "be polite," act as if we didn't catch a nasty whiff, and adapt to the stink. Unfortunately (especially in faith-based circles), we are prone to ignore the problem. *I mean, we are Christians, after all. We need to avoid confrontation whenever possible.* In a manner of speaking, neither do we mark the manchineel tree, nor do we uproot it.

Grace-based leadership has a very different aroma. Welcoming and warm, it wafts through the air like a warm batch of chocolate chip cookies when you've got a hankering for something sweet. Completely unsuspecting, you walk in the door and—boom! Joy of joys! Your mouth waters. Hope and delight arise as you take another deep breath and try to track the scent to its tasty source.

One more deep breath: inhale grace, exhale mercy. That is healthy leadership.

We must be so intentional about the air of our leadership. Shouldn't we crave grace-filled leadership enough to create it in our own environments? What atmosphere have we set up for ourselves and those around us? If the breath that flows through our lungs is not that of grace, you and I (and everyone around, really) may end up holding ours out of fear-based codependency. By default, the absence of grace-based attachments alongside the motivations of the 4 Deadly Ps will surface in toxically counterproductive ways.

PICK YOUR POISON

From person to person, the outworking of fear can look very different. Though many of its expressions seem harmless, codependency can do untold damage to any system it infiltrates. As leaders, you and I simply cannot afford to overlook the implications this has on our organizational structure, leadership style, and relationships.

Most of the time, we each pick our poison unaware. But if you and I don't pay attention to what we are ingesting, the deceptive appeal of this fruit could choke the life out of us. To toy with codependency's toxicity is to underestimate its potency. Whether the symptoms are subtle or shocking, the influence of fear always brings harm—this is just how our brains work. Apart from a conscious effort to combat it, the poison of codependency will course through our ranks.

Like manchineel tree sap, codependence is ruthless in its precision to burn, injure, and kill those exposed—especially a leader's character. Hidden best by an appealing appearance, powerful personality, or compelling vision, it does its damage. Not surprisingly, some common characteristics of a dynamic leader can make it extremely hard to detect. Especially at first, the best of us may find ourselves too easily drawn in. But usually it doesn't take long before we notice the scarcity of grace, joy, and shalom.

POWERED VERSUS POISONOUS LEADERSHIP

The contamination of fear and codependency builds up. The nature of codependency is like that. Over time, it will choke the life out of any leader, team, and ministry. Cultures permeated with fear-based human wisdom, strategies, and tactics may accomplish good things but fall short of God's kingdom. As Scripture says, "Flesh gives birth to flesh, but the Spirit gives birth to spirit" (John 3:6 NIV). At some point our human approach will fail. Though God can use such efforts to do good things, the goal is to bring *His* kingdom to earth. Not. Our. Own. After all, the fruit is only as good as the tree it hangs on. If you and I are running a nonbiblical operation, it is foolish to expect a biblical outcome. As leaders, we must want God's vision more than our own. And likewise, the way we work with others to accomplish it should align with God's ways. (God's will = God's way.)

So, what does the power of grace-based leadership look like in action? Set next to its festering antithesis, grace-based codependent leadership is easy to spot. Secure, grace-based attachments shape how we relate to others, what we value, and how we lead—in good times and bad. Fear-based attachments express themselves in the same areas—only their effect is toxic. The contrast is clear: we either lead empowered by grace or poisoned by fear and codependency. Here is what it looks like:

	POWERED BY GRACE	**POISONED BY FEAR AND CODEPENDENCY**
VALUES	Value is based on grace, joy, and shalom.	Value is based on vision, mission activity, and lack of problems.
SUCCESS	Success is based on relationships.	Success is based on accomplishment or failure.
	Focus is relational and intentional in maintaining the integrity of grace-filled relationships.	Focus is on problems, and relationships are a means to an end.
IDENTITY	Identity: Who we are/group identity	Identity: What we do
	Ministry overflows from "who we are" together as a team. (It's about *us*.)	Ministry is driven by a leader's vision, tasks, and needs. (It's about *me*.)
WEAKNESS	Weakness is okay.	Weakness is hidden.
	Leaders are protectors.	Predatory behaviors create a ministry food chain. Only the strong survive.
PROBLEMS	Solution centered	Problem centered
	Problems lead to shalom and identity growth.	Problems lead to anxiety. Anxiety drives the bus.
	Problems are handled directly.	Problems are triangled.
FEEDBACK	Feedback is welcome.	Feedback is feared.

Put in neat columns, grace-based leadership is the way to vibrant spiritual transformation in our lives and communities. Let's take an in-depth look at each element of our leadership that is affected.

VALUES

You've heard it from me before: empowered leaders build everything on a foundation of grace, joy, and shalom. They hold these sacred. Since they are so important, let's review these key concepts:

- Grace is each person's identity as special and favorite.
- Joy is the delight in being together.
- Shalom is the powerful rest we experience when we know everything is right, there is nothing to worry about, and we are in the arms of one who loves us.[11]

If grace-based leadership prevails, when one of these is missing, everybody notices. (This holds true in the lives of individuals as well as in communities.) When an individual or group is unable to extend grace, joy, or shalom, the idea of pressing onward is unthinkable—at least not on a regular basis. Losing any one of these will have an impact that requires restoration before we do much else.

If this sounds inefficient or out of context in our fast-paced Western culture, just think for a minute: was Jesus ever in a hurry? People are what matters to him. Leading with attention to individual needs and capacity is consistent with His way of being. When something happens causing grace, joy, or shalom to be lost (by one or all), we should follow Jesus' lead and help one another find it again. Likewise, when grace, joy, or shalom grows, it should be celebrated and enjoyed. This kind of sustainable pace nurtures healthy strides in spiritual maturity and transformation.

The same is true for the community. Though you or I may have a high-octane style, as wise leaders we cannot use ourselves as the gauge for what everyone needs. Capacity won't look the same for everybody. In order to build group identity in and among people, we must welcome rest for both the weakest and the strongest. Purposing not to overwhelm anyone helps us become people-centered leaders—assuring that others get what they need. If necessary, we come back tomorrow to finish what we started. Leaders readily make adjustments to model and accommodate grace.

Both grace-based and fear-based leaders can be incredible visionaries. It is not an either/or situation. But if the incredible vision of an individual becomes more important than grace, it will lead to blowups and burnout all the way around. Working overseas with a global mission organization, I witnessed this sort of damage firsthand.

Ben's Burnout Methods

I arrived at the tropical headquarters, excited to teach about growing joy and peace, brain science, and recovery. The organization's leader, Ben, had a determined, hard-charging personality to match his laser-focused vision. He oozed with charisma, which made following him easy for unsuspecting recruits. Missionaries assigned to serve here rotated every two years, so Ben would drive them hard to achieve the vision he had laid out. If the vision wasn't working, he would abruptly shift gears, challenging others to pivot and get on board with the new direction.

It didn't take long before the staff pulled me aside for advice. These folks were tired, disillusioned, and burned out by Ben's approach. They told me he had made it clear that he didn't care whether he wore them out because there would be "a fresh batch of missionaries delivered soon." There was no room for discussion. As the head of this mission, Ben was proud and determined to accomplish the work God had given him to do, no matter how many workers he destroyed along the way. Undeniably, program metrics mattered more to him than God's grace, joy, and peace in the lives of people under his authority. There was nothing biblical about the situation. Ben demonstrated a lethal, nonrelational form of leadership.

No matter how incredible a visionary's aspiration, energy, and gifting may be, the goal must never be about what they or their organization is going to *do for Christ*. That is fear talking. (In this case, Ben's achievement-oriented ways were rooted in personal performance.) Mistitling personal ambition as "vision" may dress it up a bit—even convince people to gather around it, follow the leader, and "get 'er done"—but here's the thing: it will only work until people get tired, push back, express needs, or question tactics. If our highest value is not centered on God's grace, His vision will be eclipsed by our own. And that is a dangerously toxic place from which to serve.

SUCCESS

"We are all in this together." Great slogan. Revived by the recent global pandemic, this sentiment wonderfully defines success in grace-powered leadership. In this column, winning is first and always determined by the quality of our relationships. By keeping the focus here, our lives and ministry will flow. Joy, appreciation, and rest are trademarks of it and set up a win-win situation for everyone involved.

On the other hand, when we measure success by programs, projects, attendance, budgets, or other nonrelational metrics, people become nothing more than tools or problems. By *that* unstandardized yardstick, Jesus would've been considered a flop. To Him, people were never tools or projects. Building eternal relationships was His primary agenda. He didn't waste time building up His ministry platform but laid down his life to lift others up. According to the Bible, *that* is success. Lord knows, it can be slow going sometimes. But if we, like Jesus, are relationally focused, our ministry will prioritize the growth of grace-filled relationships with one another. Leading others toward life transformation, the quality of our relationships will mirror our success (or failure). The way we regard others reveals whether or not we are leading with grace.

Rich's Ruin

You've probably met a charmer or two in your day—someone with tremendous personal charisma, magnetic communication skills, and overall appeal. At one point I was working with such a man. Rich was a pastor of a rapidly growing church and a popular radio talk-show host. He was warm and caring. The man could make a sheep feel welcome in a wolf den. On the younger side of middle age, he was a really nice guy—too nice, as it turned out. I'd worked in the church counseling department. Not long after being hired, stories began to surface about a series of affairs involving Rich and several much younger women in the church for over twenty years. The revelation blindsided people. Obviously, he couldn't keep pastoring and had to step down.

Rich had built his ministry empire around his gift. So not long after he left, the staff began to eat itself alive. A disproportionate amount of energy was given to maintaining our reputation and influence in the community as we looked for a new vision or a new visionary. Departments and members of the elder board scrambled to one-up each other with their "superior" visions of the organization's future. Without any relational development among them, they readily turned on one another in competitive, ego-driven ways. Like the staff, church members quickly became divided too. Eventually, a new visionary was found. A perfect fit for the same broken model they had been using, the next pastor was power hungry and ambitious. It didn't take long before the church crashed and burned.

Let me be clear: if we stake our success on using power to achieve our goals over relationships with people, our leadership will be crippled or crushed—as will anything you or I may build in the process. Generally speaking, when a leadership team misses the foundation of grace-based relationship, they typically unite around achievement. When problems arise, goals are not hit, or someone stumbles into moral failure, the glue holding the team together will quickly lose its stickiness. At that point, things fall apart.

IDENTITY

Identity is who you and I are at the core. You remember as God would have it, our individual identity springs from the grace, joy, and shalom we come to know in the eyes of our caregivers. Healthy identity springs from attachments rich with grace, joy, and shalom reflected in the eyes of our caregivers. As we mature, our attachments strengthen, and grace, joy, and shalom multiply as we interact with others. Moving away from our family of origin (through the healthy process of individuating), you and I gradually develop a group identity with our peers. Eventually, *we* becomes more important than *me*. Though you and I don't lose our individual identities, the relationships we have with others in our community become more important than our personal ideas and pursuits. Eventually, our love for these friends becomes so great that you and I become willing to lay our lives down for these people. After all, these people are "family."

Just as with individuals, strong leadership teams take the time to grow a sense of *community* identity and help group members discover who they are *together*. For the sake of the community, we yield our own ideas, goals, and visions to one another. As we joyfully go about our ministry together, we express *our* identity—we belong to one another. When ministry flows from this sense of *we*—as opposed to *me* or the importance of *my* ideas and opinions—it represents the kingdom of God well. *He* becomes greater and greater; *I* become less and less (John 3:30).

If, on the other hand, we tie identity to what we *do*, you and I will find ourselves slowly strangling to death. Trying to *earn* our keep in a group never matured anyone, and frankly, God is opposed to the idea.

Rooted in fear and codependence, this style of leadership suffocates us in immaturity. Predictably, anytime my ideas, vision, or gifts must be the most important thing, I will have a hard time laying down my life and opinions for the greater good of my group. The team is just a means to an end.

Mateo's Mess

Years ago, I was training and consulting in a fascinating cosmopolitan city on the other side of the globe. Its diversity of cultures and ethnicities created the perfect setting for nontraditional ministry approaches. There was nothing cookie-cutter about it. Ministry here required creative agility. Enter a dynamic and magnetic ministry leader, Mateo. His Latin flare gleamed in the conservative Eurasian setting. People were drawn to him. He was fun too! He wasn't shy with his opinions either, and in a world where there were thousands of deities to choose from, the way this man talked about God made the Lord *real*, relevant, personal, and caring. This otherwise private culture readily opened up to embrace the man and his colorful ways—especially women. (You probably saw this part coming.)

Mateo had been working in the country for a couple of years before entering an affair with a woman who came for ministry. Caught in the act, he was remorseful at first. He seemed authentically sorry and willing to apologize to everyone involved—his family, his leadership team, and their ministry community. At the start, it appeared this man was well on his way to healing and the restoration of his ministry. He willingly stepped down from his position for a time, but within weeks Mateo's wife announced that she forgave him and that they had worked through their issues to her satisfaction. Very publicly, the couple started expressing their desire to be back in leadership.

Before too long, Mateo passively began to resist counseling and other elements of the prescribed restoration process. Then, he began complaining to friends and supporters in the community that he was being treated unfairly. Next, he upped his ante, claiming racial discrimination; Mateo said the leadership team was being vindictive and unreasonably hard on him. The already vulnerable staff was further wounded, as was the community they were trying to serve.

It was "all about him." Mateo's life demonstrated how *me* outweighed *we*. He cared more about getting what he needed to feel good than he did about his team. As it turned out, a trifecta of narcissism, sexual addiction, and ministry addiction was blinding him. But these were just symptoms of the deep fear below his charismatic surface. Mateo picked his poison: a selfish desire for recognition, pleasure, and validation. A preoccupation with pleasing and performing proved toxic. As far as I know, his remorse never led to repentance. Instead, it led to further damage and pain for everyone. People were just the means to the end.

Because our being is always more important to God than our doing, relationships matter more than the work at hand. Tasked with a healthy vision, a leadership team, a small group, or a family is always greater than any one person—even the leader. By moving relationally, we accomplish what He has called us to do, in the way He would do it. When you and I keep the focus on ourselves, it creates a more painful learning process than necessary. Top-down, other-centered humility helps our team *become*. To know life-transforming spiritual community, a group must become greater than the sum of its individual parts.

WEAKNESS

Grace is a potent remedy for weakness. None of us are perfect. We *all* need it, so let's get over ourselves, shall we? When the 4 Deadly Ps drive us to attach to the wrong people or things, we inherently attach ourselves to weakness. The more we resist it by trying to hide our flaws and failures, the weaker we will become. That is especially true of leaders. Call it what it is: pride. Pride attempts to hide weaknesses. Fake-it-till-you-make-it methods to cover our faults will only multiply the potential to crash and burn.

To avoid confusion, I want to articulate what I mean: I am not suggesting you expose your vulnerabilities to just anybody. Out of pride and wounding, plenty of people out there try to crush weakness when they catch its scent. But think: weak areas are where you and I have the opportunity to grow strong. Each of us must find safe people who can handle our weaknesses and struggles with compassion. The truth is, we all need grace, and God knows an honest awareness of our weaknesses will keep us dependent on Him for it. The prospect of growing relationships that welcome weakness invites new strength to my heart for us all!

Boot Camp Debacle

I worked as a senior therapist at an alternative sentencing program for substance abusers. Technically, it was a boot camp. We worked with men and women caught up in drugs, alcohol, DUIs, prostitution—things like that. At the discretion of a judge, nonviolent offenders arrived at our boot camp instead of serving prison time. Our small compound was on an old sugar cane farm near the Florida Everglades. Our offices and the living quarters were the barracks that used to house migrant workers.

In addition to the few hours of work they were required to do around the property, these clients spent most of their day in treatment. Every day, there were classes, groups, and individual therapy sessions designed to get each person the help they needed to stay sober and out of the court system in the future. As therapists, we encouraged the residents to open up and share their weaknesses with us and their peers. More than just a verbal vomit session, the therapy was carefully curated to be a safe and compassionate environment. In this place, participants could support one another as they processed various experiences of abuse and deep shame. I am thankful to say that, therapeutically speaking, our program ran separately from the corrections department. We only had to report issues that jeopardized the safety of others on the property. All else was confidential.

As beautiful as the tropical landscape was, a power-hungry poison had leeched onto the grounds in the form of a particularly angry female deputy, "Flo" (name changed for privacy). Dominance was her preoccupation. Not surprisingly, she didn't care for us therapists, but seemed to thrive on controlling and oppressing others. As anyone who has gone to counseling knows, the end of an appointment can be a vulnerable time—especially if you are doing deep, healing work. Not having done her own, Deputy Flo would hover near the door as the women left their sessions, picking up on the personal problems that had surfaced in therapy. No matter what day it was, she didn't seem to care how raw or exposed they may have felt. Invariably, Flo would use the knowledge of their issues as ammunition—loading the gun that established her superiority and kept them in line.

Flo seemed to prey upon inadequacy. She used her power to remind everyone that she was in charge, and she seemed to revel in crushing others to prove her point. Her position as an enforcer enabled her to always be "right." Consequently, everyone in her path was dead wrong. She was a tyrant. On the days she supervised the women, the deputy would frequently remind offenders of how hard *her* life had been but that *she* had never made such dumb decisions as they. It taught them not to open up and be real. (I mean, what was the point if you'd just be punished for it, right?) After a while, the therapists were tight-lipped with the corrections officers too. It was a classic food-chain setup—and the food was all poisoned. Good leaders don't sit atop the food chain consuming or crushing everyone under them like that.

I want to contrast the leadership of that deputy with one of the most exceptional people I think I've ever met, Sergeant "Daryl." Surprisingly, he worked as a drill sergeant in the same compound. While his job description required him to call inmates to comply and accomplish specific standards, Daryl was what I call "a protector." He was able to create a supportive environment around him, correcting bad behavior without breaking people down. Working through problems with the people in his charge, he seemed to have a sixth sense for when they were open to addressing their weaknesses. Though he was no pushover, the man was kind and knew how to build trust and respect. Rather than hassling and haranguing a fragile individual, Daryl would recognize the opportunity, stop, and say, "Go see your therapist." At moments like those, I had some of the most productive sessions with a person. To me, it was proof that the correction of weakness does not require crushing because of it. For all of us, addressing moments of weakness is an opportunity for actual growth. Throughout our lives, if we are healthy, you and I will discover that seeking the help of others in the areas we are weak will provide us with strength and direction.

PROBLEMS

A frequent preoccupation of some leaders and organizations is to focus on problems instead of solutions. Whenever a leader loses sight of their special and favorite identity, or that of their teammates, things will go south. Why? Because fear is hopelessly problem centered. Grace-based attachment to God and others has left the building.

It looks like this: If I am a fear-based leader and you (or your issues) get in my way, then you have made yourself a problem to be eliminated—or at least limited—and my predatory instincts kick in. I want to get rid of the disruption you are causing me and my plans. How much I get done is more important than the quality of our interactions, so your real-life problems and individual contributions just frustrate my endeavors. Even if I am a generally caring person, when I want people to be okay just so they can get the job done, something is off.

Another telltale sign of problem-centered leadership is the triangulation of conversations. Healthy leaders or team members notice when grace, joy, or shalom is missing, and they go directly to others to help restore what is missing in relationship. On the other hand, rather than go directly to another, a fear-based codependent leader uses gossip, complaining, and innuendo to influence others to do their dirty work. Those who triangulate are not interested in restoring relationships, grace, joy, or peace. They are more interested in being "right," maintaining their grasp on power, and belittling those with whom they disagree. This behavior creates division and casts blame; it insinuates all kinds of wrong and attaches it to the problem person in order to excuse any ungracious behavior on their own part. After all, if I'm in charge, it is all about *me;* this is *my* vision, and you, problem person, are thwarting it!

Maturity wise, a leader can only take a group to their own level. The fear that stunts people is only healed in community, so these dynamics must be addressed. At best, with this mentality entrenched in our culture, you and I will eventually burn out as we try to manage problems and not grow people. At worst, those in proximity will not be able to grow. If you and I want to be dynamic and effective as leaders, we always need to be working to raise up our replacement. We do that as we are discipling them—modeling a wholeness that helps heal and equip them for the role.

Becky's Blunder

I used to be heavily involved in leading recovery support groups in my area every evening. As seems to be common in such groups, one of the leaders was a woman whose husband, Will, was a recovering addict. Becky was a classic codependent. To get her husband to "behave," Becky and Will had become very involved, which allowed Becky to climb the ranks of the group structure and obtain her volunteer leadership role. Unfortunately, her growth didn't match her husband's recovery. It was as if the healthier Will became, the more Becky clamped down control. Though her desire to contribute was sincere, she was not ready to lead.

As it happens, men in the group had picked up on the vibe—they felt marginalized because Becky had such a hard time trusting them. Typically, most of the men gave up and left the group. To make things worse, none of the potential male leaders wanted to share the mantle with her. Becky had established a sympathetic tribe of women around her leadership, but the men—most of them addicts—were adrift. The group couldn't seem to get anywhere. Eventually, Becky and some members of the group recognized that the group was working well for women but not for men. They approached me, asking if I would intervene. Once I heard the story, it was easy to agree to get involved.

Especially as it pertains to the process of addiction, men need to hear from other men as they work to stay sober. My goal wasn't to take away from her leadership but to help her build her capacity to lead and experience healing. Anyone called to leadership has no choice but to do their own work first. Otherwise, any unhealed dynamics involving fears and codependency will drive things. Although it took time, over several months I began to build trust with the group, which made it easier for Becky to let me do what was needed to bring healing balance to her leadership. Once that happened, things shifted, and more men began to pour into the group. We established a foundation of grace, and a solid team comprised of both women *and* men began to rise up from the ranks.

FEEDBACK

Feedback offers you and me the opportunity to grow—as leaders, as people, and as organizations. Let me encourage you, seeking it is a powerful tool in every persuasive leader's toolbox. We must regularly and frequently seek it from our people and those we serve. Unless we have entered or constructed a fear-based system, individuals or issues that surface can be positively addressed without apprehension and with an expectation of significant gain for all involved.

I want to take you back to the story about the homeless organization I worked for in D.C. The director's name was Don. As you will remember, when we were talking about misplaced mercy, the organization's work served as an apt analogy. Though that weakness hindered their success at getting people to complete their program and become contributing members of society, Don recognized the invaluable importance of feedback. He wasn't afraid of it, and he knew that posing to be on mission would only slow them down in the long run. They were doing the best they knew how, but Don knew they needed to know more. That is why he hired me. I was brought on board as an addiction counselor but directed to spend my first thirty days assessing what they were doing well and, well, to assess what they were missing.

As it turned out, the organization just needed a programming adjustment. Because of practical constraints, if they wanted to succeed, the organization would have to decide whether they were going to serve the homeless and mentally ill or the homeless and substance addicted. They didn't have the budget or the workforce to do both effectively and sustainably. After a period of prayerful reflection, they recognized God's call for them to work with homeless addicts.

Even though it was a Christian organization, it took some time to build trust with some staffers. Before they knew me, they expected I'd be a rigid Bible-thumper who would beat people up with Scripture. After all, they'd experienced this kind of toxic Christianity in other places. That's why my main goal in the first few months was building trust and transparency. Working together, we developed a relational approach to dealing with people drowning in addiction. Within six months we established structures and programs to help deal with and transition well in our newfound reality. I couldn't be prouder of the work we did!

Since I left, the organization has stayed on the same positive trajectory. They've even developed and created a unique residential treatment program with halfway houses. They also bought a run-down apartment building, renovated it, and turned it into communal housing. The building has two hundred rooms available to those who have completed their twenty-eight-day program and are required to do a sober-living halfway house stay. Their communal housing offers built-in support services, including twelve-steps, AA, and other groups. Case managers are on-site to help residents too. At last report, more than 80 percent of people entering the program have been able to maintain their sobriety for two years or more. Wisely, the strong leadership of those men and women was not afraid to gather feedback and implement healthy change. It proved essential to the success of all they served.

As we know, codependency occurs on a spectrum. Each of us can be found somewhere on it. Because of that, you and I can expect that all systems contain some level of toxicity. Like the manchineel tree, fear-based behaviors are native to most leadership environments. Counteracting the fears that allow codependency to thrive requires cultivating robust and grace-based attachment with God and others. It is imperative we weed out the fear. As you and I begin working on our own issues, we will become better at recognizing it around us too. Though no walk on the beach, it cannot be allowed to grow and bear its fearsome fruit. When symptoms of codependency present themselves, the grace of Jesus pulls them out from the root! While fear will poison, His grace empowers.

7

The GRACES of Leadership: Values of a Grace-Based Leader

Prayer is living in vital friendship with God. Leadership is working in vital friendship with God.

—ALAN FADLING, *AN UNHURRIED LEADER*

I want to counter the common reduction of "way" to a road, a route, a line on a map—a line that we can use to find our way to eternal life; such reduction means the elimination of way as a metaphor, the reduction of way to a lifeless technology. The Way that is Jesus is not only the roads that Jesus walked in Galilee and to Jerusalem but also the way Jesus walked on those roads, the way he acted, felt, talked, gestured, prayed, healed, taught and died. And the way of his resurrection. The Way that is Jesus cannot be reduced to information or instruction. The Way is a person whom we believe and follow as God-with-us.

—EUGENE H. PETERSON, *THE JESUS WAY*

Pride makes us artificial and humility makes us real.

—THOMAS MERTON

True leadership must be for the benefit of the followers, not to enrich the leader.

—JOHN MAXWELL

J im and I first met in 2003 at a conference in Canada. I have to say that watching him over the years, he is one of the most outstanding leaders I've encountered. The man isn't flashy, doesn't jockey slick tactics, but the man is humbly *brilliant*—and pretty funny too. At the time we met, Jim lived in California and I lived in North Carolina. Crossing paths at events and talking by phone about work and life, our friendship developed. A shared love of playing music and outdoor expeditions helped further nurture a well-rounded, brother-like relationship. The two of us enjoy a bold sense of adventure when it comes to doing something new together.

Early on, Jim gave me a reading list and would field any question I lobbed his direction (Jim loves curious people). Our professional backgrounds helped us sharpen one another to the point where we began collaborating on books and workbooks together. Which leads me to "the argument appointment"—one of the genius lessons he taught me about leadership.

Several years into our friendship, we set about reprinting a trauma and addiction workbook we had written together. There was something wrong with the new layout, and we couldn't come to an agreement. All progress was halted on the project. One day, seemingly out of nowhere,

Jim said, "Ed, we need to schedule a time for a fight." *Time for a fight?* I wondered, but I went along with it. We had a conference coming up, so we both put an appointment on our calendars to meet during the first break.

Meeting in a private room, Jim and I spent the first part of our time individually quieting ourselves and recalling gratitude memories. We connected with Jesus, welcoming His presence and allowing Him to remind us of our own identity. We knew that it was essential to hear from God so we could act as a team as we reached an agreement about the workbook. The quiet created space for us to experience and resolve negative feelings together so that we could suffer well through our disagreement, act like ourselves, and be sure to keep our friendship more important than the layout problem.

I learned a lot that day. Up until then I'd never experienced anything like it. Now I wouldn't conduct an argument any other way. Jim's relational integrity embodies what I call the GRACES of leadership. The GRACES are essential core values that you and I can cultivate in our lives both to model and to enrich grace-based attachment to God and others. If they are part of our personal lives, then our leadership will reflect it too. But when gaps exist between our values and actions, problems will occur. Our values must be integrated into our life, leadership, and ministry—the core motivation for all strategy and action, from the top down.

GRACES: CORE VALUES OF GRACE-BASED LEADERSHIP

- **G**od is first.
- **R**elationships matter most.
- **A**ct as a team.
- **C**onsistent identity counts.
- **E**motions matter.
- **S**uffer well.

Let's walk through them one by one.

GOD IS FIRST.

Putting God first means that you and I keep in mind whose glory and honor we are promoting. If the honor and glory don't belong to God, then the 4 Deadly Ps drive our leadership. We all want to be liked, but when that desire dominates how we relate to others, how we work, how we parent—whatever the scenario—fear is powering the problem. If you and I aren't careful, Pleasing, Performance, Pain Avoidance, or Pleasure Seeking will seek to grab the wheel.

I know what this is like. Once, I worked for a challenging, cowboy-boot-wearing man at a rehab center. Staffing and budget issues precipitated a difficult season for the organization. Because he was its founder, he was passionate about the place and its practices. His high standards and unpredictable reactions kept the entire staff on edge; each of us spent an unreasonable amount of time worried that the swift and pointy end of his boot would be aimed our direction. At that time in my journey, I couldn't figure out a life-giving way to work for him.

Every day, I dreaded going to the office until a mentor of mine suggested a solution. "Have you thought about who you are trying to please, Ed? I could be wrong, but it seems like you are trying too hard to please the cowboy. Suppose you redirect that same energy to serve God as your primary goal. In that case, your boss won't carry the same weight in your work, and he will probably become way less important to how you feel about everyday life. If the cowboy's response is more important than God's, what is *really* going on is that *you* are trying to please *you*." Ouch. He was right.

By purposefully engaging with God first to ask what is on His heart, we seek first the kingdom—instead of the 4 Deadly Ps. It makes dealing with our codependent fears much, much more manageable.

RELATIONSHIPS MATTER MOST.

If God is first in our lives, it should show up in our relationships. Clearly, they matter to God. His Word is evidence. From start to finish, God's design for creation is relational. God created in the community of the Trinity, formed the partnership of Adam and Eve, set the stars of Abraham's descendants, and generated generations of disciples. In each case, their bonds defined their lives and legacy. Today, you and I are no different. There is no such thing as a siloed Christian life. Our Christian life is only as good as our relationships.

Because our connections with God and others matter most, you and I, as we lead, must prioritize the importance of building and maintaining grace-based attachments. As we work to fulfill our call, we must actively engage relationships—otherwise, we are missing the point. There are no lone-ranger disciples—you and I must connect in grace with others. What does *that* look like? Here are some specific questions we should each be asking ourselves:

- Are my relationships characterized by grace? (special and favorite)
- Do I feel and extend compassion toward others? (stomach-turning concern)
- As I interact with others, do I actively and appropriately demonstrate mercy? (a posture of humility and yieldedness)
- Am I harboring unforgiveness toward anyone? (grudges, resentment, hatred)
- Am I good at cleaning up my relational messes? (apologies, repentance, restitution)

You see, Jesus throws out a challenge to you and me in the Sermon on the Mount (Matthew 5). He asks each of us to consider what we are *not* doing when it comes to our relationships, particularly those with whom we are closest. Let's face it, we can all fake it pretty well when we have to, but if we pretend the bad stuff doesn't happen, the good things can't either. On a personal level, we stunt ourselves and others by ignoring issues. When you and I take the time to clean up our interpersonal messes, we demonstrate the importance of God and others.

I remember one particular test in this area. I was still in the surgical center, hooked up to the monitors, following an outpatient back injection. For some reason, my wife and I decided *this* was a good time to talk about our calendars (Mistake #1). You see, the two of us have a track record of having triggering moments when we do this. Maritza makes great plans, and I always have tons of stuff to do. As a result, life easily gets overprogrammed—and the tension snaps. Add my aggravated tone of voice to this recurring issue, and we are off . . .

We weren't making a huge stink, but my monitors were—my heart rate and blood pressure started climbing. When the nurse poked her head in through the curtain to check on me, she took one look at the numbers and, with an accusing tone, asked Maritza, "What did you do to him?" Simply put: our issues lit up the devices. My inability to take the time to quiet myself, feel compassion, and view my beloved as God does resulted in Maritza's frustration and the monitors going haywire. Right away, I knew I had made a mess that needed cleaning up. I needed to back up, apologize for my impatience, make sure she knew how deeply I loved her. In that moment, my actions needed to prove our relationship meant more to me than my schedule.

ACT AS A TEAM.

When we live with God first and demonstrate by our actions that relationships matter most to us, you and I begin to function, fit, and flow together. It is the "*we* thing"—our group identity—that Jesus is all about. *We* are all in this together, right? Who *we* are as a team (and the role each person plays) is critical to our thinking. As part of the larger group, feedback doesn't scare us—you and I are safe and accepted even when we are not perfect. After all, it is about *us*, not me.

Underscoring Jesus' direction, Paul wrote each of his epistles to churches, too—not directly to individuals. Recognizing spiritual growth was a group issue, there is an implied "y'all" in the wisdom and direction he offers. Functioning as a team serves to make you and yours more effective, and keeps you safe—especially if someone's strengths make up for your weaknesses. Have you ever seen a person who is tough balanced out by a teammate who is tender? That models the wholeness of God. Grace-based leaders connect with God and others to form and act as a well-balanced team.

CONSISTENT IDENTITY COUNTS.

You may be gathering how the GRACES build upon one another to create great leaders and environments for growth. When you and I lead the way for our team—putting God first, prioritizing relationships, and acting as a team—we help create a context for the development of grace-based identity. With time and maturity, the identity of the group and that of its members become increasingly consistent, even under challenging circumstances. Interacting with different people, groups, and conditions, we learn by example how to steadily find our true selves.

Failing to cultivate a consistent identity will cost us credibility as leaders. Have you ever seen a toddler in the checkout line, midtantrum because his mom won't buy him the candy he has been trying to grab off the shelf? This child isn't bad, but he hasn't learned to act maturely when he doesn't get what he wants. As you and I mature spiritually, we will learn how to behave when we don't get what we want (and let's face it, no one ever gets what we want all the time). If you and I don't cultivate a consistent identity, we can't model one. If we can't model one, those we lead will begin to quit trusting us. The more we connect with God and others over time, the less we will react poorly when things don't go our way.

EMOTIONS MATTER.

God created us with emotions. They aren't our enemy. Since the way we feel *does* matter, a consistent sense of identity can help us keep our emotions in check (or at least notice when they are not). Though sometimes I have to admit that the idea of feeling only positive emotions sounds pretty good, Jesus didn't model it. He felt the good and the bad.

Remember the time in the temple on the Sabbath when Jesus saw the man with the withered hand, for example (Mark 3:5)? Harnessing a close connection with His Father and compassion for the man's need, Jesus confronted the hard-heartedness of the people. The result was a groundswell of "deep distress" in Jesus. The Greek word is *orge* and literally translates as intense anger verging on rage. Jesus, gentle Savior, was enraged?! If He can feel it, is it wrong? Reading on, we learn that the Lord got so angry that he healed the guy right on the spot. (Imagine the holy boldness!) Powerful emotions—even negative ones—can motivate action. You see, it's not that we shouldn't feel unpleasant emotions. What matters is what we do when we feel them.

Through the use of functional MRI machines and PET scans, Dr. Allan Schore was able to identify six primary negative emotions that we all share:

- Fear—I want to get away.
- Anger—I need to protect myself and make it stop.
- Sadness—I've lost a person, part of my life, or something important to me.
- Shame—I'm not bringing you joy and/or you are not glad to be with me.
- Disgust—That's not life-giving.

- Hopeless despair—I lack the time and resources to deal with this.[12]

Anger and fear create an arousal state in our sympathetic nervous system that often causes us to act out in some way. The remaining negative emotions from the list—sadness, shame, disgust, and hopeless despair—suck our energy and are experienced in the parasympathetic nervous system. The emotional toll of both systems taxes us and our relationships in substantial ways—physically, mentally, and spiritually. Learning to handle negative emotions while we stay connected in life-giving ways with God and others is vital.

Processing and growing our tolerance for negative feelings is really important, and in fact, we can't do it alone. People or circumstances are bound to trigger us at some point. The cost of letting spontaneous emotions determine how you and I act is something we cannot afford. When you or I overwhelm people with our intense feelings, they will often find it hard to trust us in the future. Based on my observations, once blown up, that trust is hard to put back together. Our areas of emotional immaturity are like hand grenades with the pin pulled. Especially if we are in leadership, you and I had better know what to do with them.

SUFFER WELL.

Life is not a game of Candy Land. Stuff happens. If we learn to suffer well, it means when bad stuff happens, we can remain consistent and find joy despite our suffering. There is a sense of resiliency within. We are glad to be together. Learning to suffer well means that you and I quit looking for others to punish or blame so we can quit experiencing the pain. Instead, we remain connected to God and others to help us find our way back. Now more than ever, our culture desperately needs to see this modeled by believers of Jesus.

The Bible gives us plenty of examples. The greatest: Jesus showed us all how it's done. From His arrest at the garden of Gethsemane, through His trial, walking on the way to Calvary, on the cross, he remained the same. Hanging there, He modeled care for His mother, forgave the thief, and interceded for those who murdered Him. Are you and I ready to take this idea all the way to the cross?

Lest you think to yourself, *Sure, easy for Him, He was Jesus*, the book of Hebrews recounts how early Christians did it. They were just regular people like you and me. Knowing they had a greater heavenly reward in store, these followers joyfully accepted religious persecution, including the confiscation of their possessions.

Leaders tend to catch a lot of blame. Good leaders handle it well. If you are relatively young, let me relieve you of a common misunderstanding: just because you are doing what God wants doesn't mean that things will go well. In reality, the opposite is often true. Opposition *will* arise. The only way to navigate it is to remember grace—the Father of Jesus and the grace-based people around you know that you are His special and favorite one. Stay connected! Whatever your role or how many hours you've had behind the "leadership wheel," the responsibility is great, and it is vital to know how to handle suffering well.

The GRACES of leadership have nothing to do with being good enough or earning God's favor. They are hard-fought values designed to nurture the kind of grace-based attachment with God and others that yields a consistent and abundant harvest in life, leadership, and culture.

8 *Leading at the Speed of Grace: Practicing the Relational Shift*

G – God is first.
R– Relationships matter most.
A – Act as a team.
C – Consistent identity counts.
E – Emotions matter.
S – Suffer well.

Living in the GRACES of leadership helps to ground leaders and their teams. To abide by these values doesn't mean force-fitting a different set of gifts or establishing a new skill set. As underlying principles, the GRACES establish the rules of our spiritual road—road signs by which we can check our motivations and actions. Organizing programmatic decisions, training, and relationships around these standards helps us discover a new way of being. It starts with awareness and will change the way we think about our lives, ministry, and leadership. I don't mean that the change is an easy one, but the ideas I propose are reasonably straightforward.

Individual success implementing the GRACES requires you and me to abandon a few old-fashioned leadership paradigms. Setting aside the traditional overemphasis on strategic thinking and logical action, we opt instead in favor of what is best for the relationships we touch and the relational grace they require. Sure, the old approach works to an extent, but it is like putting low-grade fuel in a Scuderia Ferrari. A valuable Formula One car is not built to run on the cheap stuff. In fact, it will ruin the engine. Running on the GRACES of leadership, will show on the track.

If God is first in our lives and grace-based relationships matter to Him, we need to clean out anything in the system that is contaminated by the non-grace-based fuel of fear. In far too many ministry settings, the gunk of outdated leadership paradigms pollutes the lines—keeping the engine from running well. To be clear, we are not looking for perfection, but we are looking for persistence and consistency in applying the GRACES. Amidst the "Go! Go! Go!" mentality typical in our culture, you and I will find a different gear is in order. It is time to shift. The GRACES of leadership are just that: a downshift.

To God, our busyness is nothing more than noise—a revved engine with no muffler. With all we "do for God," it is ironic, isn't it? Stop long enough to remember what it was like for you when you first heard His call. Regardless of whether we were in a revival meeting or a monastic cell when it happened, there is one thing I know to be true: the authentic call of God on the life of a leader comes from a deep, shalom-centered space of grace. You'll quickly notice, every gearshift required has one thing in common: a whole and quiet connection. For many reasons, our souls need undistracted, undisturbed space; this is true for everyone, especially leaders.

Strategic plans scream to be drafted.
Messages need to be written.

Teams require training.

To-do lists shout for checkmarks.

Worship music calls for rehearsals.

And God whispers. Could it be He wants us to draw near?

RELATIONAL SHIFT TO QUIETING

Connecting quietly with God should be a leader's top priority. For most leaders, this is a significant shift. The redirection requires hard brakes and a downshift in order to make the turn. With all there is to do, it may seem counterintuitive, but if we want to be grace-based leaders, it must be our top priority. Why? Because from this lower gear of quieting, our lives and leadership gain peace, connection, and stability. Without quieting to connect, we lose time attempting to regain our sense of direction or get back into the right gear with God and others.

Isaiah 30:15–21 is a case study in the relational track the Lord wants us to drive on. A little backstory on the passage may help. At this point in Israel's history, they were a sovereign nation. They had long since left behind the yoke of Egypt and Pharoah. It was a relatively small country, sandwiched between a rapidly expanding Assyria to the north and mighty Egypt to the south. Then Assyria set its sights on Israel. God's chosen were clearly at risk and, in their fear, decided their safest strategy was to make an alliance with the pharaoh to protect themselves. Unfortunately, in the process of problem solving, they forgot to ask God first.

Many of us in leadership can relate to what Israel was going through. We see problems coming at us, and without taking time to stop and consult God, we come up with our own silly solutions. Out of fear, our hearts are far from eager and are unwilling to obey. Good thinking? Nope. The Lord makes us—and Israel—a better offer: "For the Lord God, the Holy One of Israel has said this, 'In returning [to Me] and rest you shall be saved, in quietness and confident trust is your strength.' *But you were not willing . . .*" (Isaiah 30:15 AMP, italics mine).

Scrrrrreeeeeeeeeeeeech.

Wait . . . what?

It's that last part: the "but you were not willing" warning God gave them. Of course we want the respite, confidence, and strength described here, but when you get right down to it, we also want our own agenda. When you and I are afraid, we feel safer when we are in control. We work our plans, and when we don't get what we want, our rest, peace, and confidence fly out the window. By all appearances, a lot of us quit reading past the initial promises of verse 15: "And you said, 'No! We will flee on horses!' Therefore you will flee [from your enemies]! And [you said], 'We will ride on swift horses!' Therefore those who pursue you shall be swift. A thousand of you will flee at the threat of one man; You will flee at the threat of five, until you are left like a flag on the top of a mountain, and like a signal on a hill" (Isaiah 30:16–17 AMP).

What strategies those Israelites demonstrated, eh? Good thing we aren't like them, am I right? (*wink) Sadly, a lot of today's Christians are woefully similar. Entirely counter to verse fifteen's "returning and rest," we gear around high speeds of performance and crowd-pleasing. Faster horsepower, bigger fundraising drives, strategically timed revival campaigns—is this what God is asking? If our plans are not the result of relational quiet and connection with God, we won't get the results we are after.

Quieting to connect with God serves the same purpose as the spoiler on a Formula One car. It grounds us when the dynamics around us would otherwise cause a spinout. As leaders, if we get hung up on pressing the pedal to the metal in the name of vision casting, strategizing our way forward, or problem-solving our way out of things, we will lose the race set before us. Overtly or by our outright actions, when you and I communicate to our family, our team, and the people we lead that quiet and rest can wait until the work is done and the time is right, we set up a crash for one or all.

Believe me, I can relate. For years, I followed the same work ethic. But hear me: when we make Pharaoh's protection or our plans the focus, we are rebelling against God's direction. In these verses, the Lord persists to make it clear: even a stable, earthly alliance with Egypt and all the fast horses in the world won't save them. God will have none of it. Have you ever wondered if the Lord was thwarting your best tactics and clever thinking? These verses are pretty straightforward: if we don't pay attention, He may choose to do just that. That was His promise to the Israelites here. Please notice: God never asks us for such self-motivated heroics. In reality, He is pretty clear. Returning, quietness, and rest. Period. Gracious direction comes from connection.

Therefore the LORD waits [expectantly] and longs to be gracious to you, and therefore He waits on high to have compassion on you. For the LORD is a God of justice; blessed (happy, fortunate) are all those who long for Him [since He will never fail them].

O people in Zion, inhabitant in Jerusalem, you will weep no longer. He will most certainly be gracious to you at the sound of your cry for help; when He hears it, He will answer you. Though the Lord gives you the bread of adversity and the water of oppression, yet your Teacher will no longer hide Himself, but your eyes will [constantly] see your Teacher. Your ears will hear a word behind you, "This is the way, walk in it," whenever you turn to the right or to the left. (Isaiah 30:18–21 AMP)

Specifically, God is directing you and me to prioritize time to quiet and connect with Him in order for us to enjoy all the benefits of close relationship. The process looks like this:

- **Returning to our first love.** When we stop doing "business as usual," cease striving and negotiating, close relationships with God and others will begin to develop. Returning to God—our first love—is the basis for everything. In Isaiah 30:15, the "returning" spoken of is repentance from self-reliance, plate spinning, and the pageantry of our gifting. When that truly happens, connection with God takes first place in all aspects of life.
- **Spending time with Him, which displaces fear and builds strength, confidence, and rest.** To God, an unbroken connection is the goal. As we have already established, without the priority of grace-based attachment to Him, any plans we lay and the way we lead into them will flow from fear-based motivations (approval of others, overfocus on performance, avoidance of pain, or pursuit of pleasure).

When enemies are approaching, it is natural to want to make plans. The pressure can be overwhelming. Instinctively, questions arise. It's natural to feel an urgency to find answers. *How will our church or ministry survive? How do we keep our team, staff, volunteers, congregations, and those we serve from bolting in terror? What will become of our vision? Will the funding dry up? How can we fulfill God's call in the face of the opposition?* Yet God has a better solution.

According to His Word, God says quieting and rest are the *first* place to go—this is where we are designed to live. Scripturally, to quiet is to be still and tranquil; to rest is to be calm and free from oppression and strife. When the pressure is on, if you or I think finding the solution is all on us, it will create fear. That fear may drive us to go faster and work harder. Before long we will feel the tires start to wobble. It's time to slow down before the wheels come off completely. The Lord wants to amplify the grace, attachment, and direction available to us. He calls us back to His side out of a longing to be with us. There, as He calms our fears, God restores our strength and confidence—reminding us of our identity as His special and favorite.

The secure attachment God offers you and me settles and heals our souls. Learning to quiet our bodies by connecting with Him relieves anxiety—making space for the quiet confidence and rest of Jesus. In this place, we are secure in who He has created us to be. As sincere Christian leaders, finding quiet helps us remember why we are here. Closely abiding with Jesus in this way refreshes our relationship.

- **Quieting to empower our leadership and direct our work.** Good leadership *is* hard work. Doesn't it make sense that it requires the focus of a quiet, connected spirit? God's shalom presence is weighty—embodying a peace that passes all understanding (Philippians 4:7). Quietly connecting with His divine peace builds our capacity for shalom and fuels our work.

- **Remembering that more horsepower doesn't guarantee God's power.** So which would you prefer? There is a saying out there: "If the horse is dead, dismount." When you get right down to it, many of the traditional ways we lead are unproductive. Dead, really. So why do we keep them on institutionalized life support? As leaders, such means only keep us busy and more tired. Quieting to work helps us conserve the wasted energy brought about by programmatic ventures and intellectual practices that may have worked in the past.

Ministry is not about activities. It is about relationships—first and foremost, our relationship with God. You and I may have a storehouse of gifts and abilities inside, but unsubmitted to His direction, we aren't stewarding our abilities well at all. And we are not alone. Our people are watching. Our values are showing (um . . . or not). A misguided culture of drivenness distracts many of us leaders from realizing how tired and disconnected from Him and others we actually are.

LEADING AT THE SPEED OF GRACE

If you and I lead at God's pace—the speed of grace—our lives will reflect the change. Observing when and how He moves, we can adjust our direction accordingly. A quick look at neuroscience helps us understand why leading at the speed of God's relational grace is so essential.

Left Hemisphere: Naming and Explaining
- A place of words and language
- A place of stories
- A place of descriptions
- A place of explanations, logic, and reasoning
- Very resistant to change
- Persists in the face of contrary evidence
- Open to change only when the right hemisphere is "upset"

Right Hemisphere: Knowing and Experience
- Nonverbal
- Thinks in pictures
- Interprets voice tone
- The executive control system of the brain
- Dominant for relationships, attachments, emotions, body sensations, and identity center
- Synchronizes and notices "everything"
- Decides when the left hemisphere can change beliefs

The information above illustrates how our two distinct hemispheres—left and right—function differently. In essence, they pay attention to different things. The right hemisphere focuses on relationships and attachments, emotions, and identity. It processes incoming data or stimuli first and at a speed of one-sixth of a second—faster than conscious thought. Due to the directional flow of information through our brain (right to left) and the speed at which it processes, our right hemisphere leads us to take action before the left hemisphere even knows what's happening. In other words, we're acting (or reacting) faster than we can consciously think. This speedier processing continues throughout our lifetime as our right hemisphere retains executive control over the entire brain.

Now, let's look at the left hemisphere. It is responsible for words, language, logic, and reason. This hemisphere asks questions like, *Why did this happen?* and *What does it mean?* By asking these questions, the left hemisphere helps us understand what any new incoming data or information means. We draw conclusions about both the information as well as how we just acted or reacted to it. (Remember: the left hemisphere only receives and processes data after the right hemisphere has already acted upon it!) Running at only one-fifth of a second, the left brain runs at the speed of *conscious* thought. Although this is fast, it is still slower than the right hemisphere's reaction time (one-sixth of a second). The left hemisphere is too slow to keep up with the right hemisphere and receives data only after the right hemisphere has decided what to do. A lot like the proverbial "Monday morning quarterback," the left is always playing catch-up. It analyzes and draws conclusions on what has already taken place—but does not initiate action itself.[13]

So what does this mean for grace?

When God's grace takes its rightful place in the driver's seat, our closest attachments and grace-based identity steer us in the direction of spiritual transformation. God intends that His life and voice continually direct us just as he promised in Isaiah: "Your ears will hear a word behind you, "This is the way, walk in it," whenever you turn to the right or to the left" (Isaiah 30:21 AMP). Indeed, God's direction leads us at the speed of grace!

Our closest, grace-based attachments with God and others and our identity help guide the right hemisphere to take action. You and I cooperate with His leading by quieting to connect with Him—directly and through His Word. The failure to practice disciplines of quieting and connection means that our weak attachment with God will be overwhelmed when we encounter intense pressure and fear. We don't have the capacity in place to handle the pressure. When that happens, we'll lead at the speed of fear—and try to run off on fast horses, making our own plans to save ourselves and our ministries. Weak attachments with God simply don't stand up against overwhelming pressure and fear. Strong grace-based attachments with God are the basis for leading at the speed of grace.

The need for a clear and bold reprioritization of strategies is evident. Most leadership training and approaches are based primarily on a left-hemispheric model, which is characteristic of Western thought. Heavy emphasis is put upon what we know and do. Though often impressive, the best left-hemispheric methodologies, tools, and tactics cannot compete with how God leads His people (or trained His disciples). This doesn't mean that left-hemispheric training is wrong. Left-hemispheric tools are an asset when we are learning to listen to God at the speed of grace. The only problem is the priority we give these tools. Generally, most leadership models fail to recognize the way that the brain processes information and makes decisions.

Given proper attention, grace-based connections grow grace-based identity. Both of these right-brain processes are highly experiential, so they need the left brain's help to direct and monitor things along the way. Likewise, the left brain will zoom off the track in fear without right-brain input. From a leadership perspective, we need both hemispheres in order to get where we want to go.

Why is it such a big deal? If these skills are not taught and modeled, you and I won't learn to subordinate our strategic plans to attachment with God and others. In effect, our ways are out of God's order. By prioritizing and emphasizing left-brain efforts (logically naming and explaining), we work against ourselves. We set up failure for ourselves and those we lead.

That may explain the apostle Paul's statement in Romans 7:15 (NIV), "I do not understand what I do. For what I want to do I do not do, but what I hate I do." We may know that we are supposed to love people who are mean to us as Christians, but the *feeling* of hurt or anger will come up first—before the *logic* of what we know. The left part of our brain is not able to put the brakes on the emotions of the right. Take anger, for example. Despite our better judgment, words may fly as unhealed hurts show up in chaotic feelings. Even as our left hemisphere struggles to understand why it is so upset, its explanations cannot reverse the neurological current to stop our anger. In part, that is why reading books won't stop our unfortunate reactions.

The more we connect with God and others in grace, the more hope there is for healing and transformation. Gathering new pictures, experiences, and connections in secure relationships teaches us how to do things differently. Quieting and connecting with God fuels us to handle our responsibilities and relationships at the speed of grace.

WINNING THE RACE

Quieting to connect with God tunes our personal leadership engine, strengthening our capacity to operate in the GRACES of leadership. By making it a priority, the values therein translate into concrete wins for our teams and us. Everything about how we live and lead has shifted. We are in a different headspace, and the change is noticeable. Once, metrics of measuring, monitoring, performing, and programming led the way. Now, we pay attention to thriving, grace-based characteristics. We know that we are on the right track when we spot the following relational mile markers in our ministry and among our teammates.

We welcome humility and authenticity.

Humility is a quality that invites authenticity—oversight from both inside and outside our team is welcome. Building it in from the beginning is best, but anytime will do. By proactively inviting people to give us input and feedback, you and I build trust and establish the truth that nobody is perfect. Setting such a tone for ourselves and our team makes it unnecessary to put on airs. Comfortable in our own skin, we can be our *true* selves. Real. Creating space for the weaknesses of one another encourages freedom and spiritual growth. As 1 Peter 5:1–7 (MSG) instructs us:

> I have a special concern for you, church leaders. I know what it's like to be a leader, in on Christ's sufferings as well as the coming glory. Here's my concern: that you care for God's flock with all the diligence of a shepherd. Not because you have to, but because you want to please God. Not calculating what you can get out of it, but acting spontaneously. Not bossily telling others what to do, but tenderly showing them the way.
>
> When God, who is the best shepherd of all, comes out in the open with his rule, he'll see that you've done it right and commend you lavishly. And you who are younger must follow your leaders. But all of you, leaders and followers alike, are to be down to earth with each other, for—

God has had it with the proud,
But takes delight in just plain people.

So be content with who you are, and don't put on airs. God's strong hand is on you; he'll promote you at the right time. Live carefree before God; he is most careful with you.

Notice that Peter emphasizes humility for both leaders and followers. No one is exempt. This concept is especially critical for leaders to grasp. It's grievous when leaders become authoritarian, insisting that others submit to them but forgetting that submission and humility are a two-way street. Such leaders damage the credibility of their ministry or church, wound young leaders, and take on the characteristics of a dictator more than a genuine servant-leader.

God also promises that when we are weak, He is strong (2 Corinthians 12:9–10). You and I have nothing to fear. In James 4:6, the author builds on that assurance, quoting Proverbs: "God resists the proud, but gives grace to the humble." The illusion of power is what trips us up. Some of us have learned the hard way that humility leaves us vulnerable. Yet when we lay down our power in love, aren't we most like Him? From his book *In the Name of Jesus,* Henri Nouwen offers insight on the topic:

What makes the temptation of power so seemingly irresistible? Maybe it is that power offers an easy substitute for the hard task of love. It seems easier to *be* God than to love God, easier to *control* people than to love people, easier to *own* love than to love life. . . . One thing is clear to me: the temptation of power is greatest when intimacy is a threat. Much Christian leadership is exercised by people who do not know how to develop healthy, intimate relationships and have opted for power and control instead.[14]

We encourage creativity and collaboration, not competition.

Jealousy and envy signal competition. These fruit of the 4 Deadly Ps will kill our efforts. Where did we ever get the idea someone else's creative solution or better idea diminishes us as leaders? Similarly, God doesn't want us in competition with the church down the street.

Creative collaboration is the opposite. If that is our goal, the question we need to ask is, *What does God want to express uniquely through us—as individuals, as a team, and in the broader reach of our ministry?* If we discern things rightly, competition quickly gives way to exciting kingdom purposes. Suddenly, by eliminating a competitive mind-set, you and I find ourselves empowered with creative and practical ways to carry out our calling. We can cultivate this kind of character in our communities by valuing input, suggestions, ideas, and cooperation.

We keep "vision" in perspective.

Vision is essential in leadership, and it's usually bigger than any one of us. A God-inspired vision always is. If it is worth working for, it's probably something you or I could never pull off alone. And that is the point. Our work is never about one person and his or her vision. As such, we must hold vision in perspective. It can never become more important than our relationships with people. In God's kingdom, the trick is to do so while growing a grace-filled group identity. In unity and with care, we can then boldly and clearly articulate our shared vision. That is the way our teams accomplish audacious vision.

We care about who we are together.

To do so requires that you and I consider the condition we, our team, and those we are leading are in each step of the way. Taking care to count the relational cost of what is ahead, we must plan accordingly or risk burnout. We don't organize our efforts around the strongest or the weakest but the whole group's identity. Moving ahead, we thrive. If problems or questions about what to do next arise, answers come as we answer the question, *What is best for who we are together?*

Some time ago, my farmer friend, Alan, shared something he called "the sick barn." When a cow falls ill on a dairy farm, they don't butcher her. The farmer separates her from the herd and moves her to a particular barn to recuperate. She is still a valued member of the herd. She produces milk, but it isn't healthy either. So until the cow is well again, it is thrown out.

There is something we leaders can learn here. Our group is our "herd," and herds stick by one another. We don't throw out the weak, wounded, or most damaged member of our team. Instead, it's our job to provide a merciful place for them to recover. While they are in recovery, we don't demand that they produce quality work or keep up with everyone else on the team. We give them space and time to heal. Just as the sick barn is not a permanent place for a dairy cow to live, we all need time to recover upon occasion. As leaders, we can bet that if someone always needs time in the sick barn, we are probably giving them tasks that they do not have the maturity or capacity to handle.

Our maturity and capacity levels are growing.

To be mature is to be fully developed for our age. (You wouldn't ask an infant who is learning to count her toes to help calculate a moonshot, would you?) Not reaching maturity deforms us. A mature person can maintain a sense of joy and peace even in the face of problems. As leaders, we can help recognize and grow maturity and capacity in ourselves and in members of our team. Both require careful attention. Consider: *Are there areas of my life that I know require growth? Is this member of my team up to the responsibility I'd like to hand them?* We all need wise guides to help us keep growing.

Just because we need help, expecting people who lack emotional, experiential, and developmental maturity to fill those roles is dangerous. It is crucial to weigh tasks and goals we may want to give someone against their maturity level.[15] Asking a person to take on jobs for which they lack maturity sets them up to fail. It creates unnecessary trauma, damages relationships, amplifies fears, and increases the likelihood that an individual will function from the 4Ps. Bottom line: doing so inflicts hurt. Also, somebody's "disability" may end up discrediting ourselves and others. Putting an ill-equipped person in such a position places anything we are building our ministry toward at risk. If someone needs growth in a particular area, it is an opportunity for others who are more mature to help.

The ability to control our cravings is a fundamental task of maturing. Whenever someone tries to get their needs met with sources of pseudo-joy or pseudo-quiet, immaturity is the result. The 3 Gs—Guys/Girls, Gold, and Glory—are common cravings that, if not addressed, lead to crashes. Greed, envy, and the unhealthy desire for attention are common pitfalls. We can help by not setting ourselves or others up to fall. For example, if a young leader doesn't know how to control his sexuality, putting him in charge of a counseling ministry to hurting women would be reckless. Relapse or distraction happens when people haven't completed the process of maturing appropriately. With adequate supervision and feedback, you and I can give others the opportunity to stretch and grow in much-needed areas.

We reflect grace-based identity to one another.

For both leaders and teams, reminders of our grace-based identity are key. Occasionally we all need help remembering who we are—especially when times are stressful or when our attitudes or behaviors don't line up. To do this for someone we care about is to hold up a mirror to reflect their *true* identity to them. (People with faces of grace make great mirrors.)

Unfortunately, sometimes this gets confused with "accountability," but accountability is different. Among those we lead, no one is accountable to you or me for their sins or shortcomings. Getting called out on how we have screwed up just causes most of us to hide our flaws and weaknesses. Only those who have walked with us and know our good heart can handle the responsibility. Establishing this as a norm is imperative. We need input from those inside *and* outside our ministry. You and I are wise to build in regular time with these sorts of folks. Powerful opportunities to heal and mature are at stake! That requires us to clearly define and maintain our priorities.

We keep our priorities in order.
     A while back Maritza and I were able to visit the pyramids of Egypt. At the base they are massive! Each pale limestone structure juts skyward from Giza's desert floor, narrowing more and more before reaching its pointy apex. Each ascending stone layer is smaller and weighs less than the one before it. Progressively diminishing until it reaches the pyramid's pinnacle, the weight exerted is distributed across the more substantive layers beneath. Without such a strong foundation, the weight would be crushing. The engineering genius behind these world wonders is incredible! Standing there, we realized something extraordinary about the grace that applies to all of us.

     If life were a pyramid, grace-based connection with God is the ground level—it serves as the foundation for anything that rises from there. As leaders, you and I are wise to set and model this as the footing of our lives. What follows should be equally well prioritized—marriage, family, friends, church, business, ministry, etc. With God's direction, each of us needs to establish the order prayerfully. Otherwise, we may end up constructing an upside-down pyramid—a life unable to support the crushing weight above it. Only a fool would stand near.

Ministry

Work

Church

Family

Spouse, Parents

God

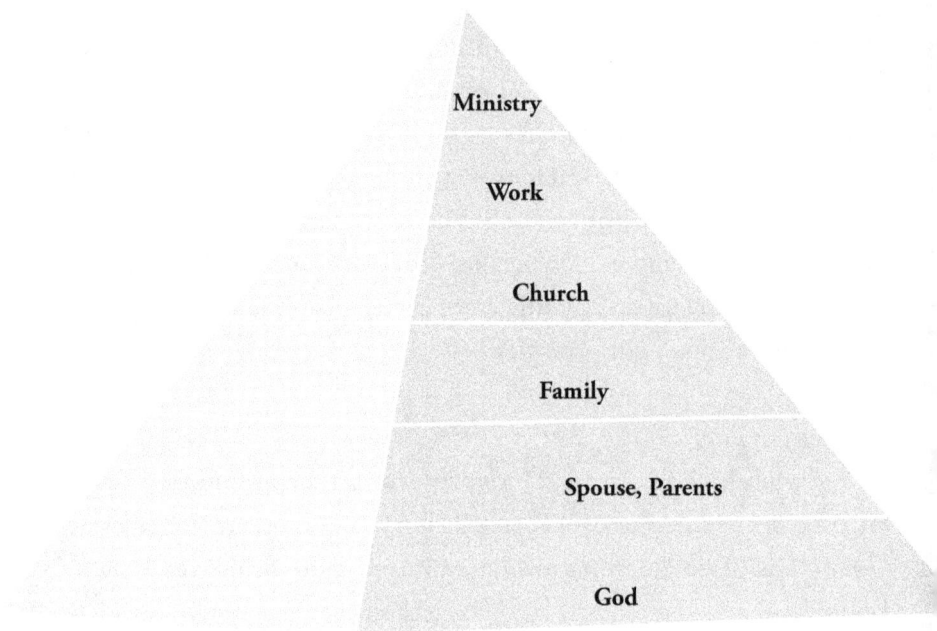

The Priority Pyramid

Having our priorities in order, starting with a strong, grace-based connection with God, is the foundation for ministry. Please understand that all of life is ministry! This pyramid does not mean to suggest that "ministry" only occurs at the top of the pyramid. Ministry includes all we do, including our connection with God, spouse, parents, family, church, work, and other forms of ministry.

Over the years, I've seen many young leaders get excited about their vision and older ones excited about momentum. That is well and good as long as these things are part of a well-ordered life. If we don't keep our priorities lined up, things will become unstable. What is truly important will get edged out. For ministry leaders, it is all too common. Swept up in other things, usually those related to the 4 Deadly Ps, we forget that life is not about our work. Most importantly, from the bottom up, life is about our relationships.

We protect others from our weaknesses.

Those in leadership must know how to protect others from our negative emotions, triggering frustrations, and strong opinions. If not, we are creating a fear-based, food-chain-like culture. The narcissistic misuse of power and authority are likely as the 4 Deadly Ps dominate, damaging our family, ministry, and team. Ultimately, leaders who don't know how to protect others become about power—who has it and who uses it.

Even on our best days, you and I can have toxic moments. We mustn't inflict ourselves on others. You and I must know when it is time to take a break.

We honor boundaries.

There has been a lot of talk in recent years about boundaries. We all need them. In order to operate in grace, you and I must be clear on our God-assigned limits—and honor them. However, what I'm talking about here is not our boundaries with others but our boundaries with ourselves.

Once, we had a stray goat who took up residence in our neighborhood. He had no sense of boundaries and enjoyed wandering from yard to yard, garden to garden, eating everything he fancied. The goat was not satisfied to stay home and eat his assigned food, nor was he content to stay and eat in only one yard. He wanted it all!

People can be a lot like goats! They roam around coveting others' gifts, anointings, facilities, families—dissatisfied to stay in their own "pasture" and fully pursue God's call for their own life and ministry. You get the picture. Forgetting their calling, mission, and team, these people run around, consuming everything in their path without asking. In order to accomplish His purpose, God has assigned boundaries that we are to operate within. A lack of boundaries indicates that the 4 Deadly Ps are in operation. Learning to live within the limits the Lord has given us is a sign of contentment. Don't be a goat.

VICTORY LANE

So, do you want your life and leadership to model the GRACES of leadership? If so, let God's unhurried pace carry you over the finish line and on to victory lane.

Relaxed, not frenzied, God's plans are for our good *and* His glory. Quietly connected with Jesus as we work, you and I enjoy the kind of Spirit-empowered living that results from hearing His voice—our grace-based relationship with Him a consistent source of guidance. Centered here, we are drawn instead of driven. Jesus takes the wheel, as they say. Steered by God's grace we discover a kind of hard work that is a good thing and the type of busyness that is fulfilling instead of compulsive. What we put our hands to becomes more creative, effective, and efficient.

Trust me, recalibrating the engine of your leadership around relationships takes self-discipline. *Most* importantly, this is something we can't do alone; we need the help of others. As such, expect it to be challenging, require intentional effort, and test your balance. Our work is to connect and stay connected so that God's love can flow out of us to others. The question is, *As leaders, will you and I give our connection with God the time and priority required?* I promise, every effort is well worth it. More importantly, in His Word to Isaiah, the Lord promises that He *longs* to be gracious to us. You and I can live and lead boldly, reassured that our tear-free eyes will behold our Teacher as we listen, learn, and lead according to His direction—at the speed of grace.

9   *Putting It All Together*

*Maybe stories are data with a soul. And maybe I'm just a
storyteller.*

—BRENÉ BROWN

B
y now you get the picture. Living connected to God is the opposite of living under the weight and ways of codependency. As
we've discovered, codependent behaviors impose burdens that
you and I aren't built to carry—bumping in line ahead of God's priorities for our lives. No matter how noble our motivation, glimmering our
goals, or big our fears, they must get in line behind the Lord's. Simply
put, God must remain first in order to guide and carry whatever is second, third, fourth, and so on.

Admittedly, it is tricky sometimes. Keeping our hearts on God's
priorities as we try to serve others, you and I may accidentally pick up
what doesn't belong to us. I worked with a leader several years ago whose
story is an excellent example of how it happens to the most well-intentioned among us.

It was a warm, sunny day, and I was looking out the window, im-
agining how nice it would feel to be outdoors. I was relaxing with a few
deep breaths as Sherry walked into the room. With a deep sigh, she

plopped down in the chair next to me and said, "Hey, can we talk for a minute?"

"Sure," I responded as I turned to face her. Instead of her usual smile and joyful intensity, Sherry sat slumped in my chair, frowning, with a furrowed brow. I immediately grew concerned. Sherry is an excellent leader and an incredible counselor. After all my years of discipling others and training leaders worldwide, she is one of the best counselors I know. This woman also has a powerful prayer life and connects with God daily during her quiet time. To say she's a veteran leader is an understatement. I don't think I'd ever seen her in such distress.

"How can I help you?" I said softly.

Sherry began unloading. "I've been working with these women for years now. These are all five highly intelligent people with incredible potential. Each is a single mom in a relationship with a husband or boyfriend who struggles mightily with sobriety. When their partners are sober, they all tell me their partner is a great guy. When he's drinking or drugging, they can't stand being around him. The fighting and yelling become so intense that they end up leaving or throwing him out. They are left to raise his child on their own.

"I work so hard with these women because I can see how the constant stress of addiction is setting their sons and daughters up for the same cycle of addicted behavior. Statistically, they don't stand much of a chance unless their mothers start working on their own recovery plan and begin making healthier choices, regardless of what their partner chooses. I've spent hours talking with these women about addiction dynamics and the need to make personal life changes. They are mostly interested in dumping their pain and anger on me and have little interest in actually doing anything about their situation. Sometimes, they rage about being deceived—again—or about his inability to stay sober. Sometimes, they grieve about the ongoing sense of betrayal. Sometimes, they vent loudly about him not being supportive or around for them or their children. Often, they tell me they are just going to move on in their lives without him. Those who do move on keep getting tangled in the same kind of relationship as the one they just left.

"They have little interest in talking with an addiction counselor, going to a support group meeting, learning about recovery, or talking with an attorney about child support. The only time they are open even to a suggestion of these things is when they are absolutely desperate and at the end of their rope. But after letting off steam by venting with me, they soon return to their normal pattern of blaming him, demanding that he change, insisting that he support them, and treating his failure with contempt. Those who do leave quickly find another relationship without first taking the time to figure out why they got themselves into such a dysfunctional relationship. It's not long before the same kind of cycle begins with the new partner. If he's not drinking or drugging, he's performing, people-pleasing, workaholic, or narcissistic. I guess they are so convinced that their 'ex' was the only problem in the relationship that they dive right back into the dating/marriage pool without a hint of insight. To make it worse, they have more children who end up back in the never-ending cycle of dysfunction."

As Sherry ended her story, she leaned forward to stare at the floor and said, "And I'm getting worn out from the dumping. Nothing changes, no matter how hard I try to intervene. It all feels like this is just too much, and it's just too painful."

She suddenly looked up, made eye contact, and asked, "What do you think I should do?"

"Sherry," I said, as I made eye contact with her. "That feels really heavy. I can see it weighing you down."

"It is," she said. "It feels *so* heavy, and I don't know what to do. I don't want to abandon these ladies because they need help. And my heart breaks for the children. They are such good kids and are trying hard, but I can see how all of this pain hurts them."

I sat back and silently reflected. Sherry didn't know it, but her situation perfectly described the kind of codependency—and misunderstanding of mercy—that precedes burnout on the part of leaders. She also didn't realize that she was leading from a place of fear—and not grace.

So I asked, "Sherry, what is the weight you're carrying in these relationships? What is weighing you down?"

"It's the pain of these women, but especially the pain of their children. I just don't want to see another generation consumed by dysfunction. And deep down, I know these women don't want that either."

"Sherry, how much of the weight you feel is about the women, and how much is about the children?"

She sat thoughtfully for a few seconds and said, "The thing that really gets me is the pain of the children and how their parents' dysfunction is setting them up."

"So, the main weight is about the children?" I asked.

"I think so."

"Can you tell me what the weight feels like?"

"Wow. I can feel it all in my shoulders and especially my stomach. It's in a knot every time I think about all of this. It's a sinking feeling that I hate because I know nothing I've said or done has changed anything."

"You sure are carrying a heavy load. It's no wonder you feel badly," I said as she nodded in agreement. My next question was gentle. "Sherry, is this weight all yours to carry?"

She stared back at me, confusion on her face.

"Let me ask this a different way. Are you supposed to carry all that weight—or do you think some of it belongs to God and to the ladies? Does it feel like it's landed all on your shoulders? Is it possible that you are carrying a weight that God never intended for you to carry? After all, trying to make sure the next generation doesn't get messed up is a hefty responsibility."

I could see the lightbulb go off in Sherry's eyes. "Okay," she said, "now I understand you. It really does feel like I'm carrying almost all of the weight here."

"Do you think there is part of this that God wants you to allow Him to carry? Is there a part of this that the women need to bear?"

"Yes," she responded. "This burden is too heavy for me. It feels very much that He wants to carry the load. I don't think I can trust these ladies to carry the load, but I do think God can carry this weight."

"So," I asked, "why is it hard for you to let go and let God carry this burden that's too heavy for you?"

"I don't know," she said. "There is something that keeps pulling back under the weight. Even now, I know God wants to carry this and that the load is too much for me. But it feels like I can't let go of the responsibility."

"Sherry," I asked, "what are you afraid of? What's the fear that keeps you stuck under the load?"

Once again, she looked at me blankly.

"Usually, as leaders, when we can't let go of a heavy load, there is some kind of fear that acts like glue between us and the weight we carry. Even if we want to and know we need to let God carry the load, fear keeps us holding on to the thing that's crushing us. So, what is yours?"

"I think," she said softly, "my fear is about what will happen to the children without me. Who will keep them from the destruction I can see coming? If I don't keep trying to help these women, what will happen to their precious boys and girls? I just can't stand another generational setup."

"So, you are afraid that without your help the children will be lost to lives of ongoing pain and failure."

"Yes," she said sadly.

"It is sad," I agreed. "I can see your compassion for these kids. Only someone with such a compassionate heart could feel so deeply about them. Your compassion is one of the things I most like about you."

Smiling, Sherry looked at me with a grin. "I'm glad you think so because right now I feel like I'm kind of a mess."

Laughing, I responded, "Well, I guess that if you are powerful enough to save those children single-handedly, you must also be the most powerful leader I've ever met. Maybe even God-like."

Sherry's smile broadened as she looked back at me with a twinkle in her eye. "Okay, I get it. I'm not God, and I can't do what only He can do."

"Bingo," I said. "I think that part of the reason you've held on to all of that weight is that, deep down inside, you believed that you could honestly save those children. When fears influence our compassion, we always take on weighty responsibilities that are too heavy and aren't ours to carry anyway. Our fears make deep compassion deadly for us and others."

"I get it," she responded.

"Now, let's go one step further," I urged. "How did your compassion, contaminated by fear, lead you to act in your relationships with these women. What kinds of things did you do to make sure the children would be okay?"

"Well," she said, "I would always be available to take their calls, even late in the evening. I would do a lot of listening to show them I cared about what they said. I pretty much let them dump when they felt the need. I listened to their rage and pain. I kept encouraging them to check out helpful resources. I even looked up healthy resources in their communities to share when we talked. I listened and offered suggestions when they talked about the children—and their baby daddy. If I didn't hear from them for a while, I'd call to check in on them to find out how they were doing. I would mail them a helpful book and recommend some YouTube videos. I did everything to help and was always available.

I sent Bibles, took their prayer requests, and prayed with them. I kept offering to be a resource to help them connect with God and begin to grow a relationship with Him. I've done everything I can do."

"That's incredible," I said. "You've been pouring your life into these women."

Nodding, Sherry agreed and then said, "Yes. But it hasn't seemed to do any good. Despite all I've done, none of these ladies has followed through with any community resources, books, videos, meetings, counselors, or Bible readings I suggested. They act interested, but they just keep pursuing the same self-defeating methods of coping. Even when they didn't want to listen, I kept showing compassion and mercy in the hopes that they would eventually hear me."

"It sounds to me like they've rejected the help."

"Yes, except for the dumping. These women seem to like using our calls and visits to dump."

"Sherry," I said with a laugh, "I don't like that. You are an awesome woman and leader. You don't look at all like a dumpster! Why are you continually allowing them to treat you like a trash receptacle?"

"Okay, I get it," she said with a broad smile. "But it felt like it was merciful and compassionate to persist, even if they mistreated me."

"But were they in a 'mercy position'?" I asked directly.

Sherry thought about it for a few moments. Remember: a person in a "mercy position" is willing to consider what others say and then respond—especially in repentance. It is the exact opposite of being "stiff-necked," which refers to someone who will not yield to God or others and has no intention of listening or changing his or her behavior. Scripturally, God resists the proud. He is quite eager to show mercy when someone is yielding, but he actively resists those who are stubborn and stiff-necked.

"No," Sherry responded after a pause, "they were not. They've been totally stiff-necked when it comes to recognizing the need for them to take any personal responsibility at all for their situation. They resist making any effort when it comes to spiritual, personal, emotional, or relational growth. They just keep waiting for their partners to change or for someone to rescue them, as long as they don't have to make any personal changes themselves."

"What does that tell you?" I asked.

"It means I've been allowing my fear to masquerade as compassion, and I've been pouring my mercy and compassion out on stiff-necked people. It's no wonder everything I tell them bounces off their foreheads like a ball against concrete. I've been misapplying mercy and hoping that something will change."

"You got it," I said. "Part of the reason you feel so exhausted as a leader is that you've been misapplying mercy. That is a sure road to disillusionment and burnout. And now, one final thing. What is in you that keeps you locked into fear and misplaced mercy? I know you fear for the children—but what's the hook in you that keeps you tied into misapplied mercy? Which of the 4 Deadly Ps (pleasing, performing, avoiding pain, or seeking pleasure) has you hooked?"

Sherry pondered this for a minute and said, "I think I want to avoid my own pain. I saw my children grow up with a lot of addiction and dysfunction in our home. I just don't want anyone to experience what I did."

"That makes sense," I said. "But what else?"

"Well," she said slowly, "I want them to like me so that I don't lose my relationship with them. If I lose the connection, I lose my influence with them and in the lives of their children. That would be painful for me. I also want to respond to them as correctly as possible so that I can help and not lose their trust. The thought that I might let them down is also painful."

"So," I said, "at least three of the 4 deadly Ps have their hooks inside you. You want to please and perform to maintain the relationships and influence you have with them. That way, you avoid the kind of pain that comes from losing either or both. It also sounds like you may be driven by the lingering internal pain of your own past experiences."

Sherry nodded thoughtfully in agreement. "Yes, I can see that. Pleasing, performing, and pain are a huge part of the way I relate to them. They are keeping me locked into fear, contaminating my compassion, and causing me to misapply mercy."

Then she looked at me and smiled. She looked lighter already. "So, what should I do in the ways I relate to them? How do I stop my codependent cycle?"

"Sherry," I responded, "I think it's time for you to have a conversation with God about your own fears. I believe He wants to help you off-load all of that weight and see yourself and your friends more clearly through His eyes. I also think He'd like to help you with the fear and pain you've felt over this. Once you see Him, yourself, and these ladies more clearly, I think you'll know what to do."

"You mean," she asked, "this isn't about just figuring out the right thing and then doing it?"

"This isn't an issue of figuring out what you *should* do. It's really about connecting with God and quieting with Him so that He can remind you of who He is, who you are, and how He sees the women you both care about so deeply. When you're seeing more clearly through His eyes of grace, you will know how to relate to your friends in a way that is life-giving for you—and them. You and God will be carrying the load together, and you'll delight in partnering with Him to love your friends as He does."

Sherry smiled and sat up straight in her chair. "Talking with God is something I know how to do. I can't wait to see what He shows me. It is going to feel great to stop carrying this weight!"

Today Sherry is a vibrant, healthy leader. Her capacity to serve God and others has hit a sustainable stride, thanks to her strong, ongoing connection with God. Talk to Sherry now, and she will attest: as good and called as you and I may be, we must beware of substituting our discretion for God's guidance. Otherwise, we will end up suffering the leadership injuries that happen when we pick up burdens that belong in God's hands. By letting Him sort out our fear-based motivations, we save ourselves from the wasted effort, disillusionment, and burnout that can result. Taking the time necessary to get to the bottom of fears that keep us stuck in unhealthy patterns, you and I can move beyond codependency and misplaced mercy. After all, God has other plans for our energies. May Sherry's story become ours.

Appendix

Codependency:
Helpful Guidelines for Change

If you're like me, when you look at codependency, it can quickly become overwhelming. Once familiar with the signs and symptoms, it seems like it is everywhere. As we begin to notice it in our lives, family systems, or culture, codependent patterns may seem insurmountable. Problems become big. Solutions seem out of reach. The cycles that swirl around us seem to easily suck us in. Live here for long and codependency, in addition to undermining our relationships, will take a heavy emotional, physical, and spiritual toll. Change is a must! But how?

Looking at codependency becomes increasingly tricky when our focus gets stuck on solving problems. Culture tells us that discovering and talking about problems is the pathway to growth, but nothing is further from the truth. While determining the depths of our codependency and talking about it does have some value, knowing about a problem is not the same thing as solving it. To begin dealing with codependency effectively, we need an approach that is solution centered, not problem centered. When you and I finally decide that this is not the way we want to keep living and are ready to shift our focus to solutions, now we are talking!

Doing that means developing new grace-based attachments with God and others that overcome fear, the 4 Deadly Ps, and codependency. These new healthy attachments will displace the role that fear and codependency play in our lives. (I write about the process of growing these life-giving grace-based attachments in *Becoming a Face of Grace*. This is where I suggest you start on your solution-centered journey.) What follows are some simple guidelines to help as you begin to address the elements of acute codependency. Remember, these are guidelines only.

1) Recognize that healing from codependency is a process, not an event.

Healing from codependency is the nature of spiritual transformation and restoration. Consequently, the process will take time. Too many Christians suffer from a "fast-food mentality" regarding healing; that is, I want it *now* and *just the way I ordered it*. News flash: neither discipleship nor recovery is instant. The more we insist on "our way," the longer it takes to deal with the roots of codependency. So strap in, leader. Get ready for the ride. Though it's natural to want things fast, quick, and painless, the journey of God's process lasts a lifetime. Healing isn't something we order up. But as grace becomes a natural part of our lives, we will notice the abnormal presence of fear more readily. That signals us to recognize and address codependency when it surfaces.

2) Refocus on the proper goal.

In the early stages of codependent recovery, it is essential to remember the goal: we want to shift our focus and energy away from someone else or the presenting problems. For example, that may mean moving your attention away from one of the following:

- the overwhelming workload that keeps you from time with your family

- the desire to perform well enough to keep a troublesome deacon board happy
- the urge to placate a difficult but influential congregant
- the sense of responsibility for the pain and problems of those who come to you for help

Instead, an excellent place to begin is to ask the Lord, *What is my actual responsibility here? What is your perspective on this, Jesus?*

As you and I grow a grace-based foundation in our life and leadership, we recover the mental energy that we have been giving away. A couple of principles are necessary to help us refocus our attention.

a) **The Bombshell Theory.**[16] It is mind-blowing how this blows up unhealthy patterns. The theory is this:
   - I cannot change another person by direct action.
   - I can only change myself, by the grace of God.
   - Others may tend to change in reaction to my change.

   The Bombshell helped revolutionize my life. I began to realize that well-intentioned efforts to change people, problems, and situations around me are doomed to fail. Rooted in fear, my old approach cost me dearly in terms of emotional, physical, and spiritual health— leaving me dangerously close to burn-out. The Bombshell Theory helps me remember that I'm responsible for me.

b) **God-centered prayer: a change in the way we pray.** Too many of us have been taught to offer up "other-centered" prayers to make our problems or problem people change. We may pray things like this:

- *God, change my spouse. Help him quit drinking so he is not so unpredictable and explosive.*
- *Lord, please change this person at church who is making my life miserable.*
- *I can't stand my elder board, Jesus. Please make them behave.*

What we really need is to redirect the object of our petitions. Practically speaking, to begin our recovery from codependency, you and I must ask God to change us. Some examples may help clarify what I mean:

- *Bring about the change in* me, *Jesus.*
- *I'm in desperate need of transformation in this area of* my life*; please help* me.
- *Father, I know I can't change these people and their problems. Will you help change the way I am reacting to them?*

See the difference? A humble, bravely grace-rooted prayer of surrender yields wisdom and peace.

Made famous by Alcoholics Anonymous and other twelve-step programs, the words of the Serenity Prayer are a prayerful plea for three critical elements of the Lord's discernment and guidance in our lives. It provides a definite shift in mental energy. Through this prayer, we center ourselves and circumstances on God's provision of peace, courage, and wisdom. "God, grant me the **serenity** to accept the things I cannot change, the **courage** to change the things I can, and the **wisdom** to know the difference."

3) Ask for help.

No part of our spiritual journey should be a solo mission—especially the journey of recovery. We cannot heal codependency on our own, so you and I need trustworthy people and resources in our lives who will respect our privacy and confidentiality.

    a) **Join a grace-based small group to help grow secure attachment and identity.** Because grace-based attachment with God and others displaces fear-based behaviors, becoming part of this kind of group is vital. (For more specifics about the characteristics of such a group, read *Becoming a Face of Grace*.) Celebrate Recovery, Al-Anon, and other similar groups follow a twelve-step process of recovery. (If a group setting is not for you, be sure you find a counselor who specializes in twelve-step recovery.)

    b) **Consider talking with a counselor who specializes in work with codependency.** Ideally, you or I may prefer a Christian counselor with this expertise. In many situations, one may not be available. If that is the case, a secular counselor who specializes in codependency will help clients look at life from a fresh perspective, challenge fear-based beliefs, and help plan a practical recovery strategy.

    c) **Share your situation with a trusted friend, mentor, or advisor.** Remember: gossip kills recovery, and not everyone is a wise guide when it comes to complex issues, so be discerning.

    d) **Learn all you can learn about codependency.** There are some excellent resources out there. Melody Beattie's *Codependent No More* and Pat Springle's *Untangling Relationships: A Christian Perspective on Codependency* are just a couple.

4) Detach.

Now the process of refocusing has begun. As we move toward recovery, it is time to turn our attention to the essential and often misunderstood detaching process. Detaching means letting go of the chains that keep you and me locked into the pain, problems, and behaviors of others. Stuck in codependency, the pain of others becomes our pain. Their problems become our problems. We obsess about their negative behaviors and the pain we are doomed to feel due to their actions. In essence, we bolt our chains to the bottom of their emotional elevator and allow them to push the buttons. When they are up, so are we; and when they plummet, we do too—just hoping we don't get crushed.

Whether personally or as leaders, detaching is vital in recovery. It allows us to break the bonds that keep us firmly fastened to the crazy behaviors, moods, whims, and opinions of someone else. Christians sometimes struggle with detaching because of the incorrect assumption that it means separation or divorce. That is not accurate and stems from a complete misunderstanding. Detaching allows us to pick the lock. Bottom line: do you and I want to remain cuffed to dysfunction, or would it be better to attach to God and others in grace?

Once our hands are free, you and I can take hold of God's grace. Our attachment to Him becomes more secure, and our objectivity about another person or situation also improves. Scripture describes our liberation in Christ: "For in Him we live and move and have our being" (Acts 17:28). When you and I codependently pursue the 4 Deadly Ps, we usually end up living, moving, and having our being in other people in order to please people, perform, avoid pain, and pursue pleasure.

Another aspect of detaching means we realize our inability to control other people, cure them, or cause them to behave differently. We recognize that we are not all-powerful and that God is the only one who loves another person perfectly. He can work in someone else's life in ways no one else can, including you and me. Each of us has limits, and we do best when we live within them. When you and I come to terms with the idea that God is sovereign, we can let go of our inappropriate expectations, misplaced weight, and misguided attempts to control others. The detaching process frees us to walk in the robust life and identity that only comes from Him.

5) Establish structures for safety.

As you and I ask for help and begin to detach, it is crucial to start considering the people and situations in our life that make healthy recovery impossible. Healing from a wound or wrong-doing is tough if we are in an unsafe situation where the injury is ongoing. (Imagine trying to recover from a bad burn if someone is still holding a lit match close to your skin.)

By establishing structures for safety, you and I create the space we need to begin to stay safe and heal. Physical, emotional, sexual, verbal, spiritual, and (sometimes) legal limits keep us and others safe. Well-defined limits can help us see things clearly and without emotion. Such parameters are not intended for use as retaliation or revenge and can be modified as conditions change. Establishing these structures will require the help and support of groups, mentors, counselors, etc. (Important note: report abuse immediately.)

6) Remain connected with God and His grace.

We must learn several practices in order to abide in Him:

a) **Talk with God about your fears.** Rather than engage with an unhealthy person or situation, talk with God about your fears. Many Christians are afraid to—mistakenly believing that fear is bad, and God would be upset with them for feeling it. This idea is foolish. God knows our fears and would love to be with us and share a conversation about them.

b) **Find peace and move from it.** God intends for the kind of peace that comes from a grace-based attachment to Him to be the GPS that guides our lives. Amid the chaos that surrounds codependency, God's peace is crucial.

In the New King James translation, Colossians 3:14–15 tells us, "But above all these things put on love, which is the bond of perfection. And let the peace of God rule in your hearts, to which also you were called in one body; and be thankful." Here, the word *rule* means to act as an umpire or referee. In other words, God intends for His peace to direct us always as we move through our recovery from codependency.

c) **Stay out of "enemy mode."** Enemy mode is a nonrelational state wherein we fail to see another through eyes of grace, and instead view him or her as an adversary to conquer. Reject the weapons of control, manipulation, toxic shame, revenge, gossip, and the urge to self-justify. Connected with God, you and I live in His peace and love our enemies.

7) Check your vision.

In order to grow in grace and remove codependency from our lives, we must gain new perspectives.

a) **Learn to see God, ourselves, and others through His eyes.** In recovery, this is the way you and I begin to change. Second 2 Corinthians 5:16–17 gets to the point: "Therefore, from now on, we regard no one according to the flesh. Even though we have known Christ according to the flesh, yet now we know Him thus no longer. Therefore, if anyone is in Christ, he is a new creation; old things have passed away; behold, all things have become new." We want to see others with eyes of grace.

b) **Look for planks before splinters.** Living in codependency, we tend to focus on other people in an attempt to fix their faults, ease their pain, or make them behave. Typically, this method backfires. To see people this way is to judge them by their own problems and malfunctions. When this happens, you and I lose sight of our own recovery issues.

Matthew 7:3–5 has a lot to say about how we can learn to see ourselves and other people correctly: "And why do you look at the speck in your brother's eye, but do not consider the plank in your own eye? Or how can you say to your brother, 'Let me remove the speck from your eye'; and look, a plank is in your own eye? Hypocrite! First remove the plank from your own eye, and then you will see clearly to remove the speck from your brother's eye."

Jesus had a great sense of humor! The word *plank* literally refers to a kind of large beam used to build a house. In essence, He's saying, "Hey, get that load-bearing six-by-six out of your forehead, and you may be able to help the person next to you with the splinter in their eye." (You may notice your headaches go away too.)

8) Healing and forgiveness are important.

In order to be released from our codependent relationships, we must pursue both healing and forgiveness, of others and ourselves.

a) **Seek healing.** Healing is the process of removing blockages in my life that keep me from grace-based connection with God and other people. Sometimes these obstructions are the result of something that you've done to hurt yourself or those around you. Other times, the blocks may be the consequence of something that has been inflicted upon you.

Whatever the case, there are many approaches to healing. Some are more Christ-centered, while others are not. Over the years, I've learned a few things. In my experience and practice, it is essential to keep the focus on connecting with God. He will guide and direct the process, removing whatever hinders our ability to live fully in Him and with other people. Another important learning? Deep healing almost always requires the assistance of a grace-based guide.

b) **Make forgiveness a priority!** As you and I work on codependency, God knows forgiveness doesn't come easily. Often, Christians want to jump into forgiveness too soon. As a result, they end up forgiving on a superficial level, one that does not lead to wholeness and healing. In my experience, before we can forgive others from the heart, guidelines like those described here must be followed. As you journey into recovery with Jesus, He is sure to lead you to the depths of forgiveness. Cooperation with His process and timing is essential.

9) Consider your overall health.

Because codependency takes an emotional, physical, mental, and spiritual toll in our lives, here are a few good questions to ask:

- *When was the last time I went for a physical?*
- *Is my current lifestyle balanced and sustainable?*
- *Is the way I am living promoting wellness or damaging my body?*

10) An important note about reconciliation.

In the process of resolving codependency, reconciliation is one of the fruits, not the root of it. Just like our desire for forgiveness, we are often way too eager to push for this critical stage. Maybe it is because we fear losing a relationship or position. But be aware: pushing for reconciliation too quickly can irreparably damage relationships, ultimately rendering it impossible.

As we work toward recovery, an important thing to be aware of is that there are two kinds of reconciliation in the end: one is guaranteed, the other is not. Let's look at them both:

- The first kind of reconciliation happens when you and I are reconciled by grace to God and begin to put on our new identity in Christ. As that happens, we increasingly live, flow, and interact with others—at peace with who God made us to be. As we reconcile the specifics of who we are in Jesus, the kingdom advances better through each of us. Guaranteed.

Trust me: the work is worth it! You and I can rest assured that the deep healing and the growth we experience will impact the kind of relationships we form in the future. On both personal and leadership levels, our healing will affect the way we respond to people in the future.

- The second kind of reconciliation involves the restoration of healthy relationship with another person. Mutual reconciliation requires us each to participate in our own recovery and healing process. If we've been part of a codependent relationship or system, we each have to do our own work. You and I don't get to control what that looks like or how long it takes, but rest assured, it cannot be rushed.

Whatever the story, if you and I do our respective recovery work and others don't choose to do their own, fear not. The new relationships we have in the future will change and improve. No longer will we be stuck in unhealthy cycles of relationship—and this freedom is change for the better! Above all, as we pursue the process of our recovery from codependency, a sharp focus on connecting with God will guide us toward the healing, forgiveness, and reconciliation He desires in our lives.

Endnotes

1   Barna Group, "Christians on Leadership, Calling, and Career," Research Releases in Culture and Media, June 3, 2013, https://www.barna.com/research/christians-on-leadership-calling-and-career/.

2   Barna Group, "The State of Pastors: How Today's Faith Leaders Are Navigating Life and Leadership in an Age of Complexity" January 26, 2017, https://barna.gloo.us/reports/the-state-of-pastors-self-leadership.

3   Ibid.

4   Ibid.

5   Barna Group, *The Porn Phenomenon: The Impact of Pornography in the Digital Age* (Ventura, CA: Barna Group, 2016), 80.

6   Carl Lentz, "Our time at Hillsong NYC has come to an end," Instagram post, @carllentz, November 5, 2020, https://www.instagram.com/p/CHONe5ODr9z/?utm_source=ig_web_button_share_sheet.

7   Warren, "The History of Pie," EverythingPies.com, accessed November 19, 2021, ://www.everythingpies.com/history-of-pie/.

8   Dallas Willard, *Living in Christ's Presence: Final Words on Heaven and the Kingdom of God* (Downers Grove, IL: InterVarsity Press, 2014), 95.

9   "Cancer Facts & Figures 2021," Cancer.org, accessed December 14, 2021, https://www.cancer.org/research/cancer-facts-statistics/all-cancer-facts-figures/cancer-facts-figures-2021.html.

10   Pat Springle, *Untangling Relationships: A Christian's Perspective on Codependency* (Merritt Island, FL: Search Resources. 2003), 10.

11   E. James Wilder, Edward M. Khouri, Chris M. Coursey, and Shelia D. Sutton, *Joy Starts Here*, (East Peoria, IL: Shepherd's House, 2013), 14.

12   E. James Wilder and Edward M. Khouri, *Restarting Workbook* (Pasadena, CA: Shepherd's House Publishing), 41.

13   For more information on this topic, refer to *Joy Starts Here* by E. James Wilder, Edward M. Khouri, Chris M. Coursey, and Shelia D. Sutton or *Rare Leadership* by Marcus Warner and Jim Wilder.

14   Henri Nouwen, *In the Name of Jesus: Reflections on Christian Leadership* (Chestnut Ridge, NY: The Crossroad Publishing Company, 1989), 59–60.

15   For additional information on this topic, read *Joy Starts Here*, chapter 4, by E. James Wilder, Edward M. Khouri, Chris M. Coursey, and Shelia D. Sutton (Pasadena, Shepherd's House Inc., 2013).

16   Dunklin Memorial Church, *The Family Recovery Process Workbook* (Okeechobee, FL: Dunklin Memorial Church 1991), 25.

www.ingramcontent.com/pod-product-compliance
Lightning Source LLC
Chambersburg PA
CBHW022055020426
42335CB00012B/697